PRAISE FOR

The SAVORING THE OLDE WAYS series

A SEPTEMBER *to* REMEMBER

". . . here, as in other places, [Bumpus] also sends us on a sensory tour with her descriptions of the marvellous meals they enjoyed, of course all handmade, regional, and accompanied by superb wine. A true celebration of Italy. I believe that Carole Bumpus is such a successful author because of the love and passion she puts into her books, through her writing the landscapes, architecture, and gastronomy of Italy are brought wonderfully to life. Highly recommended!"

—*Susan Keefe, TheColumbiaReview.com*

"In *A September to Remember*, I was transported to Italy and gratefully sank into the story of Carole Bumpus' real life adventure into culinary and cultural heaven. Her skill as a storyteller shines as she guides the reader into a world of tradition, sensuality, joy, and celebration, immersing you into the rituals, colors, and flavors unique to Italy. I truly felt like I was there! The bonus: excellent recipes in the back of the book."

—Linda Joy Myers, President, National Association of Memoir Writers, Author of *Song of the Plains* and *Don't Call Me Mother*

"Abundant with Italian culinary traditions of ritual and region, this delightful travel memoir charms and entices. Bumpus is genuinely present in her stories, as if reliving the experiences in real time. . . . Bumpus extends a gracious invitation to join her, with delectable, regional recipes—a shared feast that brings her journey home to us."

—Kate Farrell, author of *Story Power: Secrets to Creating, Crafting, and Telling Memorable Stories*

"This is a must have guidebook for those people (and that includes me) who plan a trip to Italy. The author's humor fills the pages with great hints of do's and don'ts. Written with poetic description, the book is a dash of travel memoir, a dollop of history, and a taste of cuisine. And to enhance the Italian Table, Bumpus ends the book with scrumptious recipes."

—Cheryl Ray, Author, *Spirited Voices: Marauders (emagazine)*,
Fault Zone Anthology: A Sea Shift of Mind, and *Sail: Blow Out at
Johnson's Lee – Sail magazine*

"How much can one experience in a one-month sojourn through the Italian South? Quite a bit obviously. This delightful read takes us to commonly visited destinations as well as on roads less well travelled. Along the way we are introduced to history, local cuisines and traditions as well as entertained by a free flowing, often witty, account of the joys and frustrations of foreign travel."

—John Pinto, *Professor Emeritus, University of California, Riverside*

"As you would expect (from Bumpus' previous works), we learn a lot about the food . . . experienced in different parts of the country. But this book is much more than that. Carole makes you feel like you're there with her. If you want to learn about Italian history, culture, and food, then *A September to Remember* is a book for you."

—Lloyd Russell, booksage.blogspot.com

SEARCHING *for* FAMILY *and* TRADITIONS
at the FRENCH TABLE, BOOK TWO

"The author's straightforward narrative delivers vivid imagery of both the surroundings and the people. . . . An engaging gastronomic presentation of French history and culture."

—*Kirkus Reviews*

"Bumpus's attention to detail creates a rich sense of people and places. . . . The food that Bumpus tastes and writes about is unforgettable, thanks to the array of included recipes with unusual names. . . . Eloquent and packed with history, geography, and recipes, *Searching for Family and Traditions at the French Table: Book Two* is a melting-pot text––a travel memoir that's concerned with cuisine and culture too."

—*Foreword Clarion Reviews*

". . . her conversational style easily draws the reader into the experience. An enjoyable book for those interested in France, WWII, and French food."

—Judy Alter, Story Circle Book Reviews

"Bumpus weaves wonderful stories into her adventures. But, at the same time, she gives her readers fly-on-the-wall glimpses of ordinary family life, and the opportunity to savour with her the incredible cuisine of France. Whether you love France, enjoy discovering new things, want to try some of the traditional recipes at the end of this book, or just want a thoroughly enjoyable read, I highly recommend this book!"

—The Good Life France

SEARCHING *for* FAMILY *and* TRADITIONS
at the FRENCH TABLE, BOOK ONE

"Both a regional history and a cooking memoir, this is even more than the sum of its parts, and a celebration of living life every moment. Francophiles, history fans, and foodies will love this book."

—*Booklist*

"Mouth-wateringly delicious, evocative, and utterly charming."
—French Book Worm, on Good Life France.com

"These are stories of history and change, of cherishing traditions partly because of the sense that they may not continue forever, making them even more precious and Bumpus' recording of them even more vital. . . ."

—Jeannette Ferrary, author of
MFK Fisher and Me: A Memoir of Food and Friendship

"Carole's enthusiasm for the region's people, history and culinary traditions leaps from the pages in this down-to-earth exploration of north-eastern France. Pull up a chair, pour yourself a glass of wine and dig in!"

—Fiona Valpy, author of *The French for Love*

"Warning: Do not read this book if you are hungry or within reach of a credit card. You will end up cooking (and eating) all of the included recipes, or buying a ticket for the next flight to France, or both—all while devouring this book. Because, much like the dishes and stories she describes, Carole Bumpus's writing is simply delectable."

—*Pink Pangea*

A SEPTEMBER *to* REMEMBER

SAVORING THE OLDE WAYS SERIES

A SEPTEMBER *to* REMEMBER:
SEARCHING *for* CULINARY PLEASURES *at the* ITALIAN TABLE

◦ BOOK THREE ◦

Lombardy, Tuscany, Campania, Apulia, and Lazio (Roma)

by

CAROLE BUMPUS

SHE WRITES PRESS

Published 2021
Printed in the United States of America
Print ISBN: 978-1-63152-727-2
E-ISBN: 978-1-63152-728-9
Library of Congress Control Number: 2020917548

For information, address:
She Writes Press
1569 Solano Ave #546
Berkeley, CA 94707

Book design by Stacey Aaronson

She Writes Press is a division of SparkPoint Studio, LLC.

Years ago, before the love of my life was known to me, I would often profess that "the only trips I take are 'guilt' trips." Since my marriage to Winston Bumpus, the doors to my world have been thrown open, as travel is one of the many endeavors we enjoy sharing. From treks back and forth across the Colorado Rockies in the VW camper to summer vacations in Cape Cod to forays to Europe, we've discovered our "almost always best selves" in each other's company—all, while traveling.

As it turns out, this was especially true in 1998, when I retired as a family therapist, throwing off the shackles of work, and my dear husband suggested we travel to Italy for a month. It is with great delight that I've shared that journey, which could never have taken place without his encouragement, in these pages.

I dedicate this book to him—Winston Bumpus—for being the spark that ignited my love of travel and fostered my deep and abiding interest in other cultures, peoples, and the celebration of life through food. It was this specific adventure that awakened my desire to capture the stories we were told and to begin a new career as a writer. Again, his belief in me and his encouragement of my efforts have been the catalyst. I am most grateful to him.

∽⚬∾

CONTENTS

☙

Campania

❧

Recipes from the Chapters

FRANCE

SWITZERLAND

GERMANY

Aosta
Val
D'aosta

Como

Trentino-
Alto Adige

AUSTRIA

Turin

Lombardia

Milan

Piedmont

Friuli
Venezia
Giulia

Liguria

Veneto

Padua

Genoa

Venice

SLOVENIA

Emilia-
Romagna

Trieste

MONACO

Bologna

CROATIA

Florence

SAN
MARINO

Corsica
(France)

Toscana

Grosseto

Umbria

Le
Marche

Adriatic Sea

Sardinia

Rome

Lazio

Abruzzo

Ponza

Molise

Tyrrhenian

Naples

Campania

Sea

Amalfi

Puglia

Basilicata

Ustica

Brindisi

Palermo

Aeolian Islands

Calabria

Mediterranean Sea

Sicilia

Catania

N

0   50 mi

0   50 km

PROLOGUE

While traveling abroad, have you ever strolled down a cobblestone street, passed an open window, and heard laughter flowing out to greet you? Have you ever stopped to listen to the banter while wondering what it would be like to live there? In that house? That village? And, oooooh! What are those wonderful aromas? Well, you were not alone. I have too.

For me, it all began in Italy. When my husband and I decided to take a month to travel throughout Italy, I had just retired as a family therapist. I had made no specific plans for my future, which was a good thing, because this trip changed my life. Once I danced in the streets of the first *festa*, I was hooked. As soon as I tasted the foods so lovingly prepared by the locals, I knew I not only wanted to learn their recipes, but I also wanted to understand more about the people. And as a lover of traditional foods and of home cooking, I discovered a very key element: traditional foods bring European families together in a manner not experienced in the U.S.—not only for holidays, but for every day of their lives.

My book series, *Savoring the Olde Ways*, is part culinary memoir and part travelogue, and is derived from a compilation of intimate interviews, conversations, travel notes, and recipes I had the good fortune to gather along those very cobblestone streets.

My deepest thanks go to all those who readily opened their doors to share their most intimate stories and family traditions with me. And, to those dear translator friends who accompanied me on my "treasure hunts" of a lifetime, I am forever in your debt. You taught me to appreciate the importance of family and regional traditions and to never take anything for granted. Learning a recipe in one region is never the same in another region, village, or even at a family table. Embrace the difference and the nuances. And follow your nose!

A SEPTEMBER *to* REMEMBER:

SEARCHING *for* CULINARY PLEASURES *at the* ITALIAN TABLE

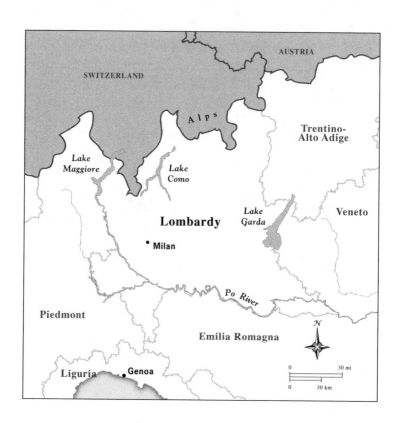

CHAPTER ONE

When in Mi-Lano, Buy Mi-lanese

*T*he plane bucked and shuddered over the tops of the French Alps before sweeping down over the snow-filled valleys of northern Italy. Foreboding clouds swirled about the plane obscuring our only view of Milan before we dropped like a rock into our descent. On the ground, we were rushed into a queue that stretched across the tarmac as rain began to fall.

This was the first day of our month-long dream vacation to Italy. It had been a crisp September morning in 1998 when my husband, Winston, and I left San Francisco, and after hours in flight and more hours of delays in Frankfurt, we finally arrived on a small plane in Milan. Sleepily, we forced ourselves to quicken our steps as we were herded like a gaggle of geese into the Milano Malpensa Terminal.

Knowing little Italian, we realized our disadvantage as we cocked our heads forward to catch the sharply delivered announcement in *Italiano*. We had no clue what was said. Too exhausted and bleary-eyed to focus, I figured I would deal with the language thing later—or so I thought.

Standing in the baggage terminal, which must have stretched for miles, we scanned the carousels for our bags. As we lumbered along, I noticed a river of luggage—I mean it—a river of dust-covered luggage which was cordoned off from arriving passengers. Dates scrawled across the baggage surfaces were from weeks earlier. Questions softly pricked at my semi-conscious mind, but it did not dawn on me then that I, too, might be forced into an imaginary boat to cross this River Styx in order to find my bag. Yes, the big bag that held every bit of clothing I had packed for our month-long journey.

Once it was clear my suitcase had not made the flight, I nonchalantly waved my hand and said to Winston, "*Allora! Non c'è problèma!*" (the only Italian words I knew at the time). "They'll find it and deliver it to our hotel." Confidently, I strode into the airport office to file my claim, in triplicate and without a word in English, where I realized it was actually a very big *problema*. The immense office, with long lines at each of the five open counters, gave rise to a newly discovered anxiety. *Will I ever see my bag again?* My bag was only one of perhaps thousands—maybe millions—of lost bags this office handled annually. My heart sank. No matter. The officials were cordial, seemed efficient, and were very encouraging. Plus, we were exhausted. After an hour of standing on one foot and then the other, we finally made our way through another queue to find a taxi.

I would like to say I remember *seeing* the city of Milan on our drive to the hotel, but the truth is I only *heard* the city of Milan. The heavens opened with a vengeance and rain began a deafening tattoo on the roof of the car obscuring our view on all sides. All the while, the taxi driver happily bellowed at top volume over the techno-music he had blaring from his radio. He expertly navigated the stream-swollen boulevards and we arrived at our hotel only somewhat scathed.

The hotel room was lovely with a wide balcony overlooking the city and, upon pulling back the draperies, the sun, for an instant, broke through the clouds. We caught our first glimpse of the magnificent spires of the crown jewel of Milano, the Duomo—one of the three largest and most beautiful Gothic cathedrals in all of Europe. Yes, we would visit her the following day.

After a long shower, I stepped out of the tub refreshed. At that moment it hit me: I had nothing clean to put on. My husband, being the accommodating sort (and who had all *his* suitcases), offered me a pair of his briefs. I hesitated, but finally succumbed. I had no choice. (And, ladies, I must admit I found his underwear quite comfortable.) I strutted about in front of him, modeling his black cotton undies as they caressed my bum.

Win, ever the one to take command, with a flick of his hand and a swagger to his step, said, "When in Milano, buy Italian!"

It sounded good to me, and even though I hated to pull my sweat-soaked slacks and sweater back on, I was confident that at least I was wearing clean underwear. (My mother would have been proud.) We headed out.

"*Sì, Sì, signora*, you're in luck," said the concierge in clipped *Italiano-Inglese* to our inquiry about a clothing store. He took me by the hand, led us out of the hotel front door, pointed around the corner, and gave me a gentle push.

Only a few small boutiques away, we found a lovely but miniscule lingerie shop. We maneuvered our way into the store where a handful of tourists and two exuberant clerks chatted. Winston, who was looking forward to speaking Italian for the first time, realized he only knew "restaurant Italian." He became mute. I crept shyly along the only aisle, picking up one pair of underpants after another. They were silky, lacy, and so soft and sensual that a tinge of embarrassment flushed my face. But I also noticed the undies were quite small and wondered if we had entered a children's shop. Just as I turned to leave, Win, who was hovering so close behind me I could feel the warmth of his breath upon my neck, ran into the back of me. At that moment, one of the shop clerks popped up across the counter from me. She held up a large pair of underpants, pointed her finger directly at me, and said in a deep-throated voice, "*Grande! Grande!*"

Well, I may not know Italian, but the message was clear. And, if I had felt a flush of embarrassment before, my face now flamed with heat. The clerk did not see me as large, but GRANDE. GRANDE. My gawd! I dared not look into a mirror, for surely my rather diminutive size (in my own eyes) had swelled during the flight. I fought back tears.

An American tourist who had been standing nearby spared me more humiliation by calmly explaining the European-size system. To further convince me, she, too, lifted a pair of underpants into the air, and in front of God and everyone, s-t-r-e-t-c-h-e-d them.

"They're wonderful," she cooed. "Simply divine!"

I cooled down to a simmer, adjusted my steamy glasses, and scanned the shop with this newly acquired information.

Winston sighed audibly, stepped out of the way, and leaned up against a counter. He pulled out his currency-exchange calculator. I thought he was glad to be out of the fray, but a small line of sweat was forming on his forehead. Had he ever been in a lingerie shop? With his head down and his fingers tapping across the exchange-rate keys, he slipped into his own element.

As I moved around the tables piled high with silken goodies, I found each item I touched possessed incredible softness. It was like touching pastel clouds—pale pink, luscious lemon, tantalizing tangerine. They were unlike anything I had ever beheld, much less worn. Once my mind seized on the notion that I, too, could wear something as fine as this—well, there was no stopping me. I scooped up a couple of bras, several pairs of underpants in assorted colors, and an exquisite white nightgown, with lacy, yet demure, qualities. Still uncertain about the necessary sizes, I looked around. My American co-hort had gone. Win, who was clearly no help in this matter, had just figured out the conversion rate and began to inhale in an uncharacteristic fashion.

Before he could utter even one wheeze, both clerks pounced upon me and ushered me into a changing room. It was the size of a phone booth. Remember those? And, for reasons beyond my comprehension, the three of us were standing inside it—together. The clerks were inciting me to undress. I am a bit shy, and I've never tried on underpants in a store—and now in front of strangers? To top it off, panic was setting in. I had just remembered that, under my slacks, lurked my husband's underwear. *Oh, gawd! Life can be so cruel!*

With actions instead of words, the clerks began cajoling me to undress while I became more and more resistant. I could barely breathe. Beads of perspiration were breaking across my forehead. I allowed them to remove my sweater and bra, as they assessed those needs, but when they began tugging on my slacks, I willed myself to out-maneuver them. I stopped their hands in mid-tug and quickly stepped into a pair of underpants and slid them up *over* my slacks. Their faces registered horror. I tried to imagine what they thought of Americans at that moment—but the deed was done. At least now I knew my new European size. Unfortunately for me, it was grande. But I decided I could live with that. Just let me out of that changing booth. I indicated my choices, and they merrily carried the items to the register.

By the time I rejoined Winston, I found him *mildly* hyper-ventilating. He had just paid for the few items and must have realized I was worth far more than even he had envisioned. My round-trip airfare had probably cost only a tad more than the lingerie. He gulped, smiled placidly at me, picked up the package, and carried it from the shop as if he were handling gold.

Yes, it was a hard-won battle, I thought, as I followed him out the door.

After that episode, my husband began to appreciate me in a whole new light. And I appreciated me, too. Terribly expensive—and sexy—underwear can do that for you. But, as a cautionary tip to any female traveler: if you are planning a lengthy trip, be certain to pack extra underwear in your carry-on. And, if ever you are in Mi-lano, buy Mi-lingerie!

Instead of heading back to the hotel, Win, whose stomach had begun to growl, steered me down the street. With the gold-plated package in hand, he turned immediately into the first restaurant he saw. It was called Altopascio and was an excellent find. Over a bottle of wine, we together devoured platters of appetizers: *prosciutto e melone* (prosciutto and melon) and *insalata mista* (mixed salad). Winston, who is never one to pass on linguine with sea food, ordered an exceptional choice: *Tagliatelle e Cozze* (pasta and mussels). For my *secondo piatto,* (second course), I opted for tender veal picatta with lemon and capers (*vitello picatta con limone e capperi*).

The next day broke with bright sunshine, setting my hopes high. Surely, my luggage would be returned. Out onto the balcony of our eighth-floor vantage point, we observed the breathtaking view of the Italian Alps to the north. Gleaming in the distance were the snowcapped mountains we had so intimately bounced ever so close to the day before. To the west of us lay downtown Milan and the Duomo, the cathedral we hoped to visit. Yes, we had done our homework for this trip and were ready to immerse ourselves in the history, architecture, art, and literature of Italy.

Milan rests in the region of Lombardy and is its capital. Grabbing my trusty tour guide, I began to read some of the historical background. "Because the streets of Milan either radiated from the Duomo or encircled it, it was widely accepted that the first public basilica built in this space dated back to possibly 600 BC. But, the first basilica, known as *basilica nova,* was dedicated to St. Thecla and was completed in 355 AD. An adjoining basilica was erected in 836. When a fire damaged the cathedral and basilica in 1075, they were rebuilt as the Duomo. . ."

"Let's get a move on," Win said, as he encouraged me toward the door. "We'll learn so much more once we are walking through it."

Of course, he was correct, so we caught a quick continental breakfast of sliced cheeses, salamis, hams, hard-boiled eggs, and blood-red orange juice. Oh, and coffee. We couldn't move a muscle without coffee. What we were to realize is that coffee is unique in every country. And Italy was not immune.

"Strong like bull," my husband said with a gasp.

A dash more cream helped me down the Cafè Americano, which obviously was made for tourists like us—but was still very bitter and strong.

"Maybe a cappuccino would be more to your liking," the waiter commented as he breezed by our table.

"I'll save that for this afternoon," I responded with verve. Yes, I had done my homework.

"*No, no, signora,*" the waiter implored. "Only tourists have cappuccino in the afternoon. And, never in evening." *I assume no self-respecting Italian would ingest café with milk after noon. But what did I know?*

Well, I could see I had a lot more to learn, but I was an eager student. You can bet I was going to pop this tidbit into my new travel journal. But first . . . grabbing me by the hand, Win led me to the front door, where we hailed a cab and headed out for a day in Milano.

Because I had just read that all roads lead to the Duomo, we decided not to fight it and went there straightaway. The splendid façade of the late Gothic-style marble exterior had been described in our guidebook as "without decoration," yet the grandeur and expanse were breathtaking. Like a giant birthday cake with delicate filigreed spires reaching up toward the heavens and dancing along the flying buttresses, it was a sight to behold. We had seen other Gothic cathedrals (the Notre Dame Cathedral in Paris, the Chartres Cathedral in France, the Westminster Abbey in London, and the Salisbury Cathedral in England), but no cathedral is without its own unique history, exterior, and décor.

Deep in the guidebook, I discovered a quote from Mark Twain, who in *Innocents Abroad* wrote of his visit in 1867 to the Milan Duomo: "What a wonder it is! So grand, so solemn, so vast! And yet so delicate, so airy, so graceful. A very world of solid weight, and yet it seems . . . a delusion of frostwork that might vanish with a breath!"

We made our way through one of the five portals graced with magnificent emerald-green bronze doors as Mark Twain continued to put my thoughts into words: "The central one of its five great doors is bordered with a bas-relief of birds and fruits and beasts and insects, which have been so ingeniously carved out of the marble that they seem like living creatures—and the figures are so numerous and the design so complex, that one might study it a week without exhausting its interest." And we were not even past the front door.

So, let me take a solemn moment here to point out that we were about to embark on the first of what would become one of our many docent-led tours of Italian historical churches, muse-ums, cavernas, grottos, ancient cities and more. Little did we know then that the word "tour" would become another four-letter word for us, but I digress.

Making our way on to an English-speaking tour, we began, with nose to stone and marble, the exploration of the interior of the cathedral. According to the guide, the history of design and construction of this colossal wonder, which can hold up to forty thousand penitents, began in 1397 by Visconti. Great dispute ensued as the church began to look like the out-of-style Gothic works of the French. *Che brutta!* How hideous! But, by taking on the late-Gothic design, the building of the Duomo was a struggle that continued over the next five full centuries.

The interior alone was well over four hundred years in the making. In 1488, both Leonard da Vinci and Donato Bramante proposed competing with designs for the central cupola. But it was Ludovico Sforza who completed the octagonal cupola and decorated the interior with four series of fifteen statues each, portraying saints, prophets, sibyls, and other biblical figures. This massive interior, we were told, reflects the rules of the Counter-Reformation and is in the form of a Latin cross with five naves. The central one is double the size of the others and comprises a transept with three naves and a presbytery flanked by two rec-tangular sacristies. (Ah, but that is too much information. Even for me.) Though you might like to know that fifty-two giant clustered columns divide the space and are crowned with capi-tals and lined with niches holding statues of the saints and the prophets. The stained-glass windows, which lends the vast space a kaleidoscope of colors, were decorated with scenes from the Bible. The marble and stone floors were begun in the fifteenth century and not completed until the mid-twentieth century. All aspects of this cathedral show the effort devoted over the many centuries to the completion of its magnificent design.

For a breather, our group was taken by an *ascensore* (elevator) to the rooftop terrace for a closeup view of spectacular sculpture that would otherwise be underappreciated—alas, not even noticed from the ground floor hundreds of feet below. The view from this vantage point was of both the mountains we had seen from our hotel and the plains that spread out below us and beyond the city limits of Milan. The roof was truly a forest of openwork pinnacles and spires, which were delicately balanced on flying buttresses. Like a parade of larger-than-life carved saints, seraphim, and angels, all marched up and down for only those on the rooftop to behold. The ornate and intricate octagonal lantern that stood like a crown atop the Duomo was topped with a spire which brought the total height of the entire church to 356 feet. And, poised at the pinnacle, was a gilded statue of the young Madonna reigning overall. Again, Mark Twain said it all: "They say that the Cathedral of Milan is second only to St. Peter's at Rome. I cannot understand how it can be second to anything made by human hands."

Yes, for some of us this was a complete marvel. But I learned later that not all had the same reaction. Oscar Wilde, who visited Milan eight years later in June 1875, wrote in a letter to his mother: "The Cathedral is an awful failure. Outside the design is monstrous and inartistic. The overelaborated details stuck high up where no one can see them; everything is vile in it; it is, however, imposing, and gigantic as a failure, through its great size and elaborate execution." I'm thinking he was a man afraid of heights and had failed to make the trip to the rooftop. Each person must judge for themselves, but for me the vast array of highly detailed sculptures almost brought me to my knees.

Completing our tour, we decided to search for lunch. We walked across the Piazza del Duomo to the north and through the porticos into what we discovered was the famous Galleria Vittorio Emanuele II. One of the world's first shopping malls, this incredible four-story building, constructed of two glass and iron arcades, again in the shape of a Latin cross, is between the il Duomo and Teatro alla Scala. Built in the Renaissance-revival architectural style, this arcade houses some of the most exquisite of cosmopolitan shops and boutiques such as Prada, Gucci, and Louis Vuitton. This building was begun in 1865 soon after Italy became unified. In fact, when it was completed, it was named after the first king of Italy, Vittorio Emanuele II, in 1867, who was in attendance at the grand opening.

Finding ourselves in such elegant surroundings, we decided to eat at Café Biffi. It was one of the first restaurants to open in the Galleria and was known for its famous *Ossobuco alla Milanese* (cross-cut veal shanks with vegetables and wine) and *Risotto alla Milanese* (risotto made with plenty of aged Parmigiano-Reggiano cheese and saffron). We chose one of each and gorged ourselves on those not-so-light-weight dishes accompanied by glasses of wine. It was then that we realized the wine can sometimes be more expensive than the dishes. Ah, but the vino was *divino!* We enjoyed every drop.

After finishing our *pranzo* (lunch), we began to feel a bit logy. Possibly jet lag was creeping in—or the heavy lunch and wine. We made our way further down through the Galleria and out into the streets, where we gazed up at one of the most famous of all opera houses in the world: La Scala. If we had had energy, we might have made our way to the ticket booth to purchase tickets. Or, for that matter, sussed out the dining hall of the monastery of Santa Maria delle Grazie, where the original Leonardo da Vinci's "Last Supper" was located. But no.

Instead, the nagging thoughts of my lost luggage persisted. We took a cab directly to the airport and made our way back to a group of cheerful baggage handlers. Alas, we came away empty-handed. And my spirits were dashed. Even though Win continued to encourage me with the thoughts of a whole new wardrobe, I knew we were headed into the hinterlands of Tuscany for several weeks and would be staying in—not a city; not a town; not even a village—but a farmhouse at a wide spot on the road in southern Tuscany. The only clothing available was from a farmer's market. I wondered if they carried *grande*. Morosely, I made my way back to the hotel with Winston trying to cheer me up. Definitely, a nap was in order. Quite honestly, I don't recall dinner, but we never miss a meal. So, I assume we rose to the occasion.

As we were checking out of the hotel on our second morning in Milan, the receptionist called out to my husband, *"Telefono! Aeroporto! Telefono, per favore, Signore! Aeroporto!"*

"No thank you," Win said politely. *"Treno.* We are off to catch the train."

Within minutes we would be heading out the door and down the street, dragging his luggage and my pathetic little overnight bag to the train station for our journey south to Tuscany. I had given up hope and figured my peripatetic suitcase had absolutely joined the River Styx of luggage at the Milan airport. But the receptionist forced the phone into my husband's hands. *"Aeroporto* for you. They have found your suitcase."

Win took the phone and within moments looked at me with a most perplexed smile. "They found your suitcase and want us to pick it up at the airport."

"But we have no time," I exclaimed. "We will miss our train. And we are being met in Grosseto." Moments of exasperation like this leave me weak. I slumped onto my husband's suitcase.

"Not to worry, love! I gave them our forwarding address. They will deliver it tomorrow!"

"In Tuscany? In Poderi? Do you think they can find us?"

"Hope so," Win said, as he eased me off his suitcase. He began to whistle as he strode out of the lobby and headed onto the cobblestone streets toward the train station."Coming?" he called out over his shoulder.

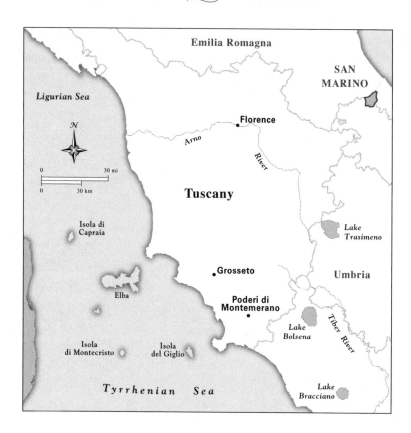

CHAPTER TWO

Festa di Poderi di Montemerano

uring our six-hour train ride from Milan, down through Genoa and along the shimmering coastal waters of the Tyrrhenian Sea, my head bobbed on and off Winston's shoulder. My thoughts kept the beat of the moving train—click-clack, click-clack, click-clack—as I breathed a sigh of relief for my hopefully-found bag. With fondness, I thought of how this trip to Italy had come about. Winston and I had spent the last few years studying the "classics" with a Stanford professor at night school. His class, *Making of the Western Mind*, had opened our minds to everything from Homer to Hemingway, including history, art, and literature. Our interest in Italy had been deeply whetted by the professor who believed that the "classical center of the world" or the "belly button of the universe" emanated from Florence. So, when I spotted an ad in a San Francisco magazine for a rental of a "charming, Tuscan farmhouse, deep in the hills of Etruria," we had no choice but to answer it.

I recalled the word *Etruria*—*(É-trur-iya)*—letting it roll off my tongue as I dialed the Bay Area number. I knew little about Italy, much less Tuscany, except in the classical sense, but the provocative sound of *Etruria* resonated through my head.

Win and I soon found ourselves seated in a small San Francisco coffee shop across the table from the owner of the ad. Lisa was a quiet woman, mid-fifties, modest of dress with a gentle, unassuming manner, who held us captive with her piercingly blue eyes and beatific smile. She wore no makeup but needed none. She was a natural beauty. But it wasn't her outer loveliness that captivated us so; it was her sense of kindness and *joie de vivre*—or whatever one says in Italian. Her voice was low and mellow, so she surprised us when she exuberantly asked, "Do you want to *visit* Tuscany, or do you want to *experience* her?" Her eyes sparkled as an eyebrow arched to accentuate her point. Her spark of drama enveloped us.

"My home is high in the hills of *Etruria* in southern Tuscany—in Poderi di Montemerano. *This* is where you will meet the *real* people." Our excitement was ignited! We sat up straighter and leaned closer.

"When are you planning to go?" she prodded.

"We were thinking September would be lovely. . ." I began.

"Ah," she interrupted, "then, you must go the very first weekend. You can attend the *Festa,* the harvest festival. You simply mustn't miss it."

As the train continued along its coastal route, I caught glimpses of snow on the mountain slopes north of Pisa. Surprised to see snow so early this far south in September, I pressed my nose firmly against the glass for a better look. Then a rail yard blurred past with palettes of white stone spread as far as the eye could see.

"Aha," I said. "That's not snow. It's Carrera marble, the same marble Michelangelo made famous with his sculptures." I patted my copy of *The Agony and the Ecstasy* in my lap. (Michelangelo's story was an enlightening influence for me.) We grinned at each other, glad the mystery was solved. We settled back into our seats but kept a watchful eye for the Leaning Tower as Pisa loomed just ahead. I must have drifted off to sleep when my husband murmured, "I think we missed it."

"Missed the festival?" I mumbled, in a fog. "That's not possible. She said we can't miss it!"

"Who said you can't miss it?" Win looked confused. "We are talking about the Leaning Tower, aren't we?"

Ignoring his question, I said, "Lisa told us, 'You can't miss the festival; it will be right on our doorstep.' Don't you remember? 'Traditional foods, music, and dancing . . . All will be there for us to enjoy!'"

"Ah, yes, and I remember the foods," he said, catching onto the change of topics. "She promised they would be *molto delizioso*." The words seemed to melt off his tongue as if he knew what he was talking about. (Had he been practicing his Italian in secret?)

"'Only made in Poderi,' she told us, 'and only for the harvest festival.' Do you remember when she asked if we liked Italian food? We couldn't answer, as we were laughing so hard."

"All she had to do was look at us. We don't miss a meal," he chuckled. We settled back wearing Cheshire cat smiles, fondly remembering her enticements.

"Come," she had said. "The festival will be a perfect introduction to Tuscany. You will revel in our beautiful hills, our delectable wines and sumptuous foods, but the people—they are the heartbeat of Tuscany. Come!" Lisa's invitation was too seductive to resist. Especially since she had arranged to come ahead and meet us at the train station. Now, that's service.

At Grosseto, a city halfway between Genoa and Roma, a flood of relief swept over me as we stepped off the train and heard a familiar voice shouting, "*Buona sera!*" and in English, "Good afternoon, Bumpuses! Welcome to Tuscany!" Lisa, along with her friend, Cecelia, embraced us like we were long lost friends, then efficiently maneuvered us out of the station and into their waiting car. Within seconds we, along with Winston's bag and my little valise, were stuffed inside a miniscule vehicle as Lisa quickly drove us out of the city traffic and into the golden Etrurian hills. The sunlight fell in diffused webs over vineyards and olive orchards and dust lay lazily across rich, *Rubenesque* fruit. I swooned. We raced on.

Our excitement intensified as Lisa, gesturing as she talked, told us, "Today is *the* day of the *Festa*." She and Cecilia giggled like schoolgirls. They had been working for days on preparations and they were excited to show us around.

After an hour's drive, she wheeled up a narrow road and parked in an open field under a banner that said *Festa*.

"There's no room to park at the top of the hill," she said, as if that was explanation enough. She helped us drag our bags out of the car and up a long hill to her house.

"I'm sure you are wondering where the village is, *si*? Well, Poderi," Lisa said, "is a twelfth century feudal term which means 'farms.' It refers to the land which was once owned by the lords of the nearby castle of Montemerano." She waved one empty hand to an out-of-sight hillside as she clutched a valise in the other.

"Only in the past 150 years have families been allowed landownership, so Poderi was never a town. It was simply a wide spot at the top of this hill where a cluster of farmhouses were built. My husband and I fell in love with the area and the people, so this is where we lived and raised our two sons. You may meet one of my sons soon."

By this point we had puffed up a steep hill and paused to catch our breath. We were sheltered by immense oak and plane trees and surrounded by overgrown vineyards. I hoped we were near the top. Soon we could see across the open vistas Lisa had referred to, and on a promontory five kilometers in the distance perched in the sunlight, was the silhouette of a medieval walled city with a square castle keep towering above all.

"That's Montemerano. And, just beyond Montemerano," Lisa said, pointing to hills beyond, "is the ancient *terme* of Saturnia. One day next week, I'll take you to the Roman baths there. It's quite relaxing."

Before she could continue, we heard a multitude of voices raise in a cheer as we rounded the final curve. Before us a raucous crowd filled the only street. We inched slowly forward, dragging our bags across the stone road past a band shell and came to a stop in the heart of the throng. Jubilant faces foisted themselves toward us. Kisses smothered Lisa, Cecilia, then us. The cacophony of voices grew, and I could barely hear myself think, much less catch Lisa's directions. She was pointing forward. Through the masses, I could make out a string of honey-colored and white stucco buildings on either side of the road. Various styles and colors of wooden shutters had been flung open as children, along with their hovering mothers, leaned out of second-story windows, laughing, and shouting to the noisy crowd below. Fuchsia-colored roses cascaded past their noses and along outside walls to brush up against the entry doors. I leaned forward to catch what Lisa was saying, as she turned and pointed again at a doorway.

She shouted over the din, "In the States we call these condos; here we call them farmhouses. You are at my home." Her face lit up. "And like I said, the festival is here, right on your doorstep."

She laughed heartily as we realized she had meant *literally* on our doorstep. She took a few steps forward before embracing one person, then another, kissing this person and that one before leading us into her home. Many hands helped us drag our bags (my husband's bags) in the door and up the stairs to the living quarters above. The lower quarters, she told us, had been relegated to storage, after the farm animals no longer shared residency.

While contemplating the concept of living with farm animals below, I walked around the main floor. The living room was open and spacious. Hewn timbers crisscrossed the high ceilings and whitewash covered all the walls. In the center of the main room was a dining table splashed with a yellow printed tablecloth. Four chairs with red-print seat cushions sidled up beneath. A stone fireplace that had served as the only source of heat for a hundred years, separated the dining room from two spacious bedrooms. We entered the bedrooms to find large windows that opened onto views of vineyards, farms, and across the way, the village of Manciano. The bathroom was compact but convenient, and the kitchen was roomy, with voices floating in the open window from the revelers below.

Back downstairs after our quick tour through her house, Lisa said, "The *Festa* will start in an hour, so rest up, as it lasts until tomorrow." She took a step out the door and into the street, where her friends awaited.

"Aren't you staying here with us?" I asked.

"Heavens, no! This is your time. And your place for now. If you need me, I'll be staying across the street with my friend, dear Margarita." Then, she was gone.

Before we unpacked, we collapsed onto the bed, hot and sticky from our day's journey and too tired to move. I dozed off, but subconsciously was aware of a low, mournful, almost Arabic-sounding chant that echoed from the street below. The sonorous male voices, deliberate and lyrical, ended abruptly with a burst of laughter and a round of applause. Another vocal utterance took up as if in response and continued with an equally vibrant cadence. Not a word could I understand. I wondered if these mournful poems were part of my sweat-soaked dreams or the reality of—where was I? Winston woke me up and we crawled off the bed to peek out of the kitchen window.

Directly below us, a multitude of faces focused intently on our doorstep, which had been transformed into a stage. A contest of sorts was being held; indeed, a poetical sparring known as a *Tuscan Contrasto*. Lisa later explained that the audience provided each team a spur-of-the-moment theme of contrasts, such as wives vs. mothers-in-law or old vs. young, and in eight-meter improvised rhyme, the men hurled their words like lances at each other. This event, performed since medieval times, signaled the beginning of the *Festa di Poderi di Montemerano*. We had awakened just in time.

Pushing through a thick gauze of sleep, we quickly sponged off, changed clothes—me, into the few new ones I had acquired—and clattered down the stairs. On the street, Lisa swept us into the crowd and began to introduce us around. This person was from Switzerland, that one from Sweden; this one from Germany, and that one from—of course, Poderi. Lisa had many friends left from her twenty years of being a resident, and they were eager to embrace their dear old friend. We immediately felt included, for they were as warm and welcoming as she had promised. And, fortunately for us, all but those from Poderi spoke English.

Then, like lava flowing down a mountain, the crowd began to surge along the stone roadway with us caught in the current. All were moving toward the festival grounds at the bottom of the hill. Smoke from the pits of braising meats tantalized us, along with the intoxicating aromas of simmering pasta sauces. The crowd turned toward the ticket booths, and the excitement grew. Music, laughter, and the banter of their melodious language filled the air. Lisa recited the menu to us in English in the most delectable detail. We hungrily placed our orders.

Another push from the crowd propelled us into nearby tents, where we were again greeted with hugs and kisses by those who were already glowing with amiability and wine. Lisa wedged us into the two remaining spaces beside her in the middle of a long table of twenty or more of her closest friends. We had barely been seated when a trumpet sounded, and the feast began. The doors to the kitchen flew open and local waiters proceeded in great numbers to the tables, carrying plates of *bruschetta*—toasted bread slathered with rich, local olive oil, chopped fresh tomatoes, and succulent olives. One simple bite brought tears of joy to my eyes. The savory yet mellow flavors danced through my mouth. Bottle after bottle of local wine began to magically appear—some from the kitchen and some from under the table.

Again, the waiters swung out of the kitchen. For the *prima piatto*, or first course, platters of fresh pasta were served. Plates of *tortelli*, Poderi's local pasta specialty—delicate pillows filled with cheese and arugula and covered with a bubbling, robust marinara sauce—were reverentially placed before us. The masses swooned with appreciation, and we joined their ranks.

Lisa leaned over and whispered, "I had to live here over twenty years before the older women of Poderi allowed me into the kitchen to help prepare their beloved *tortelli*. Yes, I could come and help at the *Festa*, but prepare the *tortelli*? Heavens, no. And the recipe? Don't even ask! It is still a much-guarded secret." She laughed with great delight.

Cecilia, who had been reserved until then, leaned over the table and shouted, "They'd perhaps have to *keel* you if you got your hands on the recipe." She grinned and sat back as handmade *gnocchi* with meat sauce and *pasta e fagioli* were whisked to their designated places along with baskets of Tuscan bread to sop up any lingering juices.

For our *secondo piatto,* sizzling grilled meats of beefsteak, pork, chicken, or sausages, all on spears, were passed down the tables. Then, *contorni,* (vegetable side dishes) of white beans, fried potatoes and mixed green salads followed the meats. Gasp!

Filled to the brim, we all leaned back to gather our collective breath, but to no avail. We were next tempted with *formaggio,* the cheese course. And the finale was the *dolci*—dessert—presented with a majestic flourish. Lisa whispered over the tumult surrounding us, "You are to choose either a *Salame cioccolata* or a *Mousse di ricotta."* We moaned with delight, though we had no idea what either contained.

"Ah," she echoed our moan, *"Mousse di ricotta* is sweet, creamy custard made by my dear neighbor, Margarita." She pointed across the table to her kindly-looking, blue-eyed friend from Germany, whom we had met earlier. Margarita nodded politely.

"Margarita made this dessert this morning using seventy-two eggs! Can you imagine that? Seventy-two eggs to make her most delectable *Mousse di ricotta!* And the *Salame* is not a sausage at all, but a rolled cookie filled with chocolate cream. This was prepared by dear Amelia," she said, pointing to a petite, gnarled elderly woman waving to us, from the far end of the table. Of course, we tried a little of each—we had to. Each was delicate, light, and almost floated off our tongues.

"Mmm," I swooned, as wine was poured into my cup, as it had been throughout the meal. Like magic, as one bottle emptied, another would pop into its place.

As the evening flowed into night, the air filled with music from a local band in the piazza at the top of the hill. The rhythm reverberated through the tents, and the crowd was on the move.

Following a festoon of colorful lanterns, people of all ages made their pilgrimage back up the hill—wizened old women in their finest black dresses, shiny from use and a heavy iron; rotund old men in their best dark suits, a bit rumpled from the lengthy dinner; young couples in sensually-loose clothing looped together with encircled arms. Giggling children in shorts and tee-shirts grabbed sweaters handed to them by caring parents; swaddled babies snuggled down in the arms of protective grandmothers; and the likes of us, middle-aged folks, laughing at shared stories while enjoying another paper cup of wine—all of us moving uphill to the beat of the music.

The instant we reached the top, the harvest moon broke out above the rooftops and sent golden light cascading onto the heads of the villagers below. Despite, or because of, the food, wine, and the beauty of the night, everyone began to dance. The music was a captivating mix of old and new, some rock and roll, some lilting Italian melodies, some familiar American pop tunes. But once the waltzes began, Winston and I stood back to marvel at the grace and elegance of the more skillful dancers. We enjoy dancing together, but on that night, we were not worthy.

"Watch for dear Mondiale," Lisa shouted to us. "He is the most exquisite dancer of them all." And there he was, the burly town butcher from Manciano, just a hillside away, guiding and gliding his partner with finesse and grace across the ancient stone street beside us.

"It is a lucky woman who dances with Mondiale," Lisa whispered to us, and a few minutes later, Mondiale had wrapped his arms about her and whirled her away.

As night became morning, the villagers, undaunted by the late hour and copious amounts of wine, continued to dance. No match for these stalwart sorts, we crept back up the stairs to our newfound home. With exhaustion cleaving to every part of our beings, we pushed open the back windows for one last peek. The moon spilled into the room and across the bed, filling the space with light. It flowed like mercury over the ancient hills and valleys and away from us. And there, silhouetted against the night sky, was the medieval fortress and clock tower, shimmering on the highest hill in Manciano. Awash with exhaustion but full of gratitude for having experienced the beauty of both people and place, we slid into bed. Our eyes flickered closed as the final songs reverberated from the streets below—or was that the heartbeat of Tuscany we were hearing?

Tortelli
Margarita Vogel's Recipe, Friend and Neighbor to Lisa Young
(No specific quantities of this recipe can be divulged,
or they will have to "keel" you.)

CHAPTER THREE

A Day in Poderi and Manciano

Our first full day in Poderi began with breakfast at Margarita's house. You remember Margarita? The one who made the seventy-two-egg dessert? Margarita had opened her lovely home across the street from Lisa's farmhouse, not only to us and Lisa and her son, Niccolo, but to Cecilia and her daughter, Camilla. And, with more friends and family visiting from Switzerland, there were at least five languages flowing through the large sunny upstairs dining room. As the jaunty group, still recovering from last night's *festa*, became better acquainted, Margarita flitted past us from dining room to kitchen and back again, her cheeks flushed, her eyes sparkling and constantly smiling.

"Margarita loves Poderi as much as I used to," Lisa said, "and she especially loves entertaining in this lovely old house!" Margarita beamed at her friend and disappeared back into the kitchen. The immense stone and wood house was several hundred years old. No one knew the exact age. The main room was a combined living and dining room and accommodated everyone comfortably. The walls were light in color and were crowned with dark beams crisscrossing the ceiling. The dark wooden floors were covered in good but well-worn rugs. Bright red geraniums grew in abundance, both in pots and in outside window boxes. With the wide windows flung open, the crisp morning air breezed in to join us.

Within moments of our arrival, we were invited to the table for breakfast which included miniature cups of espresso, (*However do they ever get those Italian coffeemakers to work?*), homemade bread toasted to perfection, Margarita's own jams, fresh fruit, plus platters of local cheeses and smoking hot *cinghiale salsiccia* (wild boar sausages). (Have you ever tasted wild boar sausages? They are quite delicious with a strong, nutty, rich flavor that is unique but not comparable to other meats. Not gamey tasting at all.)

We felt quite at home as everyone switched to English, and we were immediately privy to the local happenings of last night's *festa*. Chatter bubbled up again about how "dear Mondiale" had danced with both Cecilia and Lisa. They swooned at the telling of their late, late night dances. And was that old Leonido, a neighborhood character, who had awakened this morning comfortably seated in his battered truck just outside our door? Would his wife be coming by to retrieve him?

Amid the banter the phone rang, and Margarita disappeared. Once she returned, she announced matter-of-factly, "Your lost luggage is to be returned to you this very day!" *I couldn't believe my lucky stars!*

"How is it coming?" I asked. We were far removed from a city, much less a village, for the delivery. "How will they find us?"

"I believe they are flying your suitcase from Milano to Perugia, then trucking it over the mountains. *Non c'è problèma!*" Margarita replied. All shrugged their shoulders as if this was a daily happening. Given the hundreds of dust-laden bags I'd seen at the baggage claim room in Milan, I didn't doubt it. I breathed a sigh of relief and we continued with our breakfast and banter.

But by 11 a.m. Winston was anxious to get going. He was scheduled to pick up a rental car back in Grosseto, part of a package deal he had made for this month-long vacation. It included a thirty-day Euro Rail and Drive pass. As luck would have it, Cecilia and her daughter, who were headed home to Firenze (Florence), gave Win a lift into Grosseto to make his appointment. Now, that might have seemed like an easy proposition, but it ended up taking much, much longer than he had hoped as he waited for the rental agent to return from a lengthy three-hour lunch. *New territory. New rules.*

While he was gone, Lisa opted to stay at the house and wait for my luggage while Margarita took me under her wing. We headed into Manciano for my first experience of shopping in an Italian grocery store. (*Little did I know I had much to learn.*)

Deftly whipping into a crowded parking lot, we climbed out of the car and I looked around for the butcher shop. "Are we going to be seeing Mondiale?" I grinned. I had been told the dashing and debonair dancing butcher had a business nearby. It would be fun to see him at work. But Margarita was in a hurry.

"We might be able to see Mondiale, if we get a move on," she said, as she took a small cardboard timer from her purse and placed it on the car's dashboard. When she saw my confused look, she explained, "This timer indicates when I parked and when I plan to return to the car. Parking is tight in these villages, so you have to be mindful of others." She rushed me off to the village shops.

"Now, try to keep this straight," she said. "On Mondays, Tuesdays, Thursdays and Fridays, the town markets are closed from 1 p.m. until 5 p.m. Then, they open again for only a few hours before the shop owners head home for the evening. Store hours vary by village and by days of the week. And farmers' markets are set in each village for only one or two days per week."

"How do you know which stores are open and at what times?" I asked her, almost in a panic. I needed to stock our larder for the nine days we would be staying in Poderi, and I had no clue what kinds of food I would find. The parking timer was set to expire in only thirty minutes.

"Ah," she said nonchalantly, "you learn. Sometimes the hard way, but you learn." She smiled, grabbed my hand, and we popped into one market after another.

I have found that travel in every new country brings its own odd adjustments. At that point, my struggles included the language barrier (thankfully, Margarita spoke English well), tallying the 130,000 lire (my gawd, what did that add up to?), and the strict rules for parking. And I was also about to discover the challenges of purchasing produce (heaven forbid if you touch or fondle the fruit or vegetables on your own), selecting *formaggio* from the cheese store and buying *carne* (meat) from the friendly *macelleria* (butcher shop). (No, Mondiale was away that day. A hangover, perhaps?) Even the simple selection of dried pasta would almost bring me to tears.

Picture this: an unimaginable array of pasta shapes, and I was forced by time constraints to quickly decide between round pastas: *vermicelli, spaghetti, capellini,* and *ziti;* long, flat, thin noodles: *linguini* and *tagliarellini;* long, flat, thick pastas: *fettuccini, lasagna,* and *tagliatelle;* and short pastas: *penne, mostaccioli, ditali, farfalle, fusilli,* and *canestri.* And these were only some of the choices on the lengthy shelves filled from floor to ceiling at the *Super Mercato.*

This, all the while Margarita patiently coaxed me through the pandemonium before the 1 p.m. deadline. I inwardly whimpered, as I have enough trouble in my home market deciding between paper or plastic. In Italy, customers brought their own cloth bags.

Finally, I was ushered onto the street, where we lumbered down the hill with our arms filled with packages: sausages, pasta, fresh tomatoes, basil, eggs, olive oil, bottles of local wine, and *Parmigiano-Reggiano* cheese. I realized the importance of buying what one needs for only a day or two, max. Our car, which remained parked at the bottom of the steep hill, seemed miles away. I also remembered Lisa's tiny refrigerator would not hold all that I'd purchased.

"Oh, we must stop for fresh loaves of *pane senza sale*," Margarita said, as she spun me around.

"*Pane senza sale?*" I echoed, with no idea what that was, much less that it came in loaves.

"*Si*," she said, "those are our specialty loaves of Tuscan bread —bread that comes *without* salt. In Tuscany, our sausages and cheeses are so flavorful there is no need to sandwich them onto salted slabs of bread." She swung into the tiny shop of the *fornaio,* the baker, and we added to our purchases.

"When you first moved here, how long did it take you to figure out where you needed to shop, and what village shop was open and when?" I asked as we trundled toward the car now, also balancing loaves of bread.

Margarita laughed. "It took me quite a while, but don't worry. If you run low on anything, do as Lisa used to do. Come across the street."

"I'll bet you miss Lisa, don't you?" I asked. I knew Lisa had gone through a painful divorce after a twenty-year marriage and had spent most of her adulthood right in the house in Poderi.

"Oh, I do miss her. She was the sunshine in our entire community. Life has lost some of its luster without her; that is for certain. And this is where her two sons were born and raised. We lost not only Lisa, but her boys, as well. We felt like grandparents to them." She shifted her load and continued. "But, in a Catholic country like Italy, the treatment of divorced women is often cruel. I wouldn't wish that on her for anything."

She shook her head. "I understand that it's not quite like that back in the U.S."

"Over the years, people in the U.S. have become more tolerant, but there is always a stigma," I said. I thought of my own divorce and having to rise above the intolerance, even from my own family, but shook off those memories. Happily remarried, that was my past. I focused my thoughts on Lisa, who was still back in Poderi waiting for the return of my wandering suitcase. She had become such a dear friend to me in a short amount of time that I could only guess how painful the loss had been for "dear Margarita."

"How far away is Perugia?" I asked Margarita, changing the subject, as she drove at breakneck speed down the narrow, winding road back to Poderi.

"It's a long, long way across the mountains."

"So, I'll be lucky to get my suitcase today, right?"

"Right," she said with an all-knowing grin.

But as we pulled into Poderi, we saw a miniature truck parked at our doorway, and there on the cobblestones stood my enormous suitcase. I had not seen it for over four days. It was like an old friend who had returned, bearing gifts: fresh underwear, slacks, skirts, swimming suits, shorts, jackets, and most of my clothes for this month-long journey. I collapsed on top of the luggage and gave it a good, long embrace.

That evening we launched our first attempt at getting familiar with our little abode. Winston had found his way back to Poderi with the spiffy new rental car, and Lisa was on hand to give us preliminary instructions for using the unique water heater (high on a shelf in the bathroom).

"Under no circumstances turn it on when using the washer," she warned. Then, she taught us how to light the kitchen stove and how to use the unique dish drainer system over the kitchen sink, the Italian coffee pot, how to open the windows and shutters so they wouldn't flog against the outside walls at night, and the location of the clothes line, which, as it turned out, was just outside the upstairs bedroom window.

"Just don't fall out when hanging your clothes," she said before she loped back down the stairs. And then we were left to our own devices. Or, hers, as it were.

We proceeded into the kitchen to try our hand at preparing our first dinner. When in Italy, begin with the preparation of pasta sauce. And our pasta sauce was one of the most succulent and flavorful I've ever made—with the best boar sausages we've ever found on the face of this good earth. But, first, we opened a bottle of wine, made a toast and hooted: *Ce l'abbiamo fatta!* We did it!

At about eight o'clock that evening, there came a timid knock at our front door. There stood dear Margarita with a helping of her marvelous dessert in hand, along with Lisa. They had been concerned that we might need additional guidance, so we happily invited them upstairs where we congregated at the family table. Winston and I had just been talking about the wonderful *festa* the night before and asked if they could tell us more. We were grateful they said yes. We poured two more glasses of wine and settled in.

Margarita began by explaining some of their local history. "In every village in the Maremma, there is always, on the same date each year, a *festa*, which is a festival, also called a *sagra*, a fair. For example in Poggio Murella, the *sagra delle lumache* means snail festival; in Marsiliana, the *sagra delle fragole* is a strawberry festival; in San Martino sul Fiora, the *sagra dell'agnello* means lamb on

Easter Monday, and somewhere in the mountains, there is the *sagra delle castagne,* which means chestnut festival (of course, it's in the autumn), and so on. On these occasions, like in Poderi, people prepare food as well as dances and music. So, from spring to autumn, nearly every weekend, people travel to all these different villages as there is always something to be celebrated.

There are also the religious feasts in addition to Christmas and Easter, because every village has a patron saint that is celebrated, not only with mass and services, but also with food, dances, and so forth.

In Poderi, there are two main festivities—the *Festa di Poderi,* and the *Befana,* which is held on the eve of Epiphany, the 5th of January. It's sort of a pagan epiphany. The *Befana,* celebrated in all of Italy, is a "good witch," a sort of Santa Claus who brings sweets or coal to the children who put a stocking in the fireplace. In Poderi, the *Befana* is something very special, and she comes with her husband, the *Befano.* Both are masked (so you don't know who they are) and they go from house to house in all of Poderi, fractiously singing the *Befana* song while collecting things at each house to eat or drink."

"Does everyone join in?" Winston asked.

"Oh, my, yes! In Poderi, this event is something very special. After the *Befana* and *Befano* visit each house, the people from the house come into the streets and join the *cortège.* More and more people come together, singing while accompanied by a small orchestra. This continues for hours. At the end, or about midnight, the *cortège* enters the old schoolhouse, where everyone gathers to eat, drink, and dance till the masks fall, and only then do you know who the *Befana* couple is."

"In every house that is illuminated, the people always sing many of the fifteen verses, but especially No. 7, 8, and 9, and *riteruello.* The other verses are to be sung depending on who lives in the house: children, young people, married people, widow, or old people. If a house is dark, it will not be disturbed."

"Are the words from the song the same in every village?" I asked.

"Oh, heavens, no. The Poderi *Befana* is very special, and people from our region come to sing only our particular rendition, and, of course, to eat and drink." Margarita explained.

Lisa stood up and began to sing a few of the verses as she circled the table, again and again. It was at this moment we realized one of her other accomplishments was in the performing arts. Her lilting voice lifted our spirits and we were delighted:

7) *I Re Magi son partiti dalla parte dell'Oriente*
Con la stella rilucente e brillanti gelsomin
E nel nome
The Three Kings left the Orient afar. . . .
With the brilliance of the shining star and little brilliant "jasmine-stardust"
In the name of Maria.

8) *A voi altri <u>ragazzini</u> ho portato tanti doni*
Andate a letto e state buoni che contenti vi faro
E nel nome
For you male children I have brought many gifts.
Be good and go to bed and I will make you happy.
In the name of Maria.

9) *A voi altre <u>ragazzine</u> ho portato un bago fiori*
Voler bene al proprio amore con tauta fedelta
E nel nome
For you female children I have brought you a bouquet of flowers.
And take care of the one you love with fidelity.
In the name of Maria.

We clapped our hands as Lisa curtsied and sat back down.

"*La Festa di Poderi*," Margarita began again, "you both participated in, so I don't need to describe it to you. But, in Manciano, they have a nice tradition: *La Festa delle frasche* or *delle cantine*. *Frasche* means branches; *cantina* is a wine cellar. The festival is usually a celebration near September, to open the cellars in the *Centro storico* of Manciano. People put out branches of trees to indicate who is opening his cellar to offer wine, food (mostly *ciaffaguoni*, or cannelloni), and music. It is very nice to walk in the small streets of the Manciano hills to discover which cellar is open. Mostly you hear the music, and you have the opportunity to meet people you know.

"Since Manciano is the main city of the region, they have more festivities. For example, in summer, they have *Festa dell' Unita* and *Festa dell' AVIS*. Each festival lasts for one week, you can purchase food every evening from vendors, and they always have music and dancing. *Unita* is the former communist party, but the *festa* is not political. Everybody participates simply to eat cheap and dance. And *Festa dell'*AVIS is a fun event of an association of blood donors and then, the whole population comes out to eat, meet people, and dance. They also have a cortège with all the horses of the region and everyone walks in the streets with torches. It's always quite lovely.

The Poderi *festa* was originally a religious event. Poderi, not being a very ancient village, consists of four nuclei named after the first four families who came together here around 1700. The church and school were built together between 1951 and 1956. The church is dedicated to Santa Maria degli Angeli (Saint Mary of the Angels), which is why the *festa* took place about the 8th of September, her recognized birthdate.

"Then, it became the *festa* like we have now on the first weekend in September from Friday evening until Sunday night. The culinary part is the most important, because people from all the surrounding areas come to indulge in the local specialties, so the ladies of Poderi work very hard. The pasta must be fresh; it can't be frozen from one day to the other. That means that every morning, very early, many bags of flour and hundreds of eggs have to be worked into noodles, *tortelli* and *tagliolini*. Bags of potatoes must be peeled, cooked, and pressed to make into gnocchi. And, of course, the *sugo* (meat sauce) must be prepared fresh for each meal. The most famous *primo,* or first course, of all the festivals is found in Poderi, and it is the *tortelli,* for which there is no written recipe. Sorry! Do you have the entire menu for the *Festa?*"

I nodded, yes. "I have the full menu from last night's flyer." But, I also grabbed a paper and pencil to take more notes.

"There are foods for other holidays of the year," Margarita continued, "including a very special or traditional menu for Christmas Eve. Starting at eight o'clock, the meal continues until it is just in time to go to the midnight mass on 24th December. This is what the menu consists of:

1) A soup of *"tagliolini e ceci"* (on the *Festa* Poderi menu)
2) *Crostini di cavalfiore* (cauliflower toast)
3) *Tagliatelle con noci e miele* (noodles with nuts and honey)
4) *Baccalà con prugne* (dried cod with dried plums in a strong sauce)
5) *Frutta* (fruits, mainly persimmons which are just ripe)
6) *Dolci di Natale* (all kinds of Christmas biscuits)

"Coffee and *grappa* are included and, of course, you are served *vino della casa* (house wine). Oh, and, in between I forgot to mention salads and marinated anchovies. My husband and I used to go to the village of *San Martino sul Fiora* to our favorite restaurant before midnight mass, but now, most people eat at home."

Margarita smiled at me as I finished the notes I had been taking. I couldn't believe I had stumbled onto something so marvelous. Favorite traditions; family favorite foods. I do believe a spark was lit inside me by her descriptions. I wanted to know more. Much more.

But, at that point in the evening, we had finished the dessert and wine, and I knew we were all exhausted. We had put in another very long day.

We thanked Margarita and Lisa for everything they had shared with us—that day, that evening. And, once Winston had escorted them down to the front door, it wasn't long before we both had succumbed to a food-filled fantasy of a dream.

CHAPTER FOUR

Intervallo del Pranzo in Pitigliano
(Lunchtime in Pitigliano)

*A*lthough it was September, we awakened to a beautiful, summer-like morning. The hills around Poderi sparkled in golden sunlight and as I leaned out of our bedroom window to peek across the hills to the south, I caught sight of the castle of Manciano rising to its lofty heights as it had done since the twelfth century. We ate a light breakfast and eagerly headed out the door. This was our first day of gallivanting around Italy on our own, our first excursion in our rental car. We were excited to be heading for the ancient city of Pitigliano—a city known for its Etruscan beginnings.

As we drove along the dusty roads, we caught sight of both men and women slowly moving between the rows of grapevines, checking the fruit, tasting, and continuing along. The vines were heavily laden with bulbous grapes practically bursting to be picked. "It won't be long," we had been told. The *vendemmia,* or grape harvest, was about to begin.

Fields of brightly colored sunflowers, their yellow petals beckoning the sun to play just a few days longer, popped up among the vineyards. Their suntanned faces were tilted toward the light as if in awe, as they spent their day tracing yet again the sun's orbit along the ecliptic.

We sped past groves of silvery-gray olive trees—(yes, speeding in Italy is something we quickly learned to do)—but we slowed as we glimpsed ladders being positioned against these small yet gnarled old olive trees. We lowered the windows. Wasn't it too early in the season to harvest olives, we wondered? Is the olive season different from country to country? Nets were strung under the limbs, and yes, we could hear the resounding noise of the whack, whack, whack as the trees were being assaulted to give up their ripest fruit. *Must be the right time.*

Win pulled to a stop at an overlook before we reached our destination. Rising high above us and at the confluence of three rivers—the Lente, the Procchio, and the Meleta—stood a majestic volcanic *tufa* crest in a palette from gold to reddish brown. Tufa, porous, chalk-like limestone, formed the ancient walled city of Pitigliano—a city with Etruscan, Roman, and Medieval influences. We could not wait. Ah, but we did.

Conveniently positioned across the road was a shop tucked inside a cave. A weathered sign tilted to the side indicated—*di vino.* I made out the words, Bianco di Pitigliano, which I recalled was the name of a local wine our hosts, Lisa and Margarita, had extolled as "truly virtuous."

"Bianco di Pitigliano?" I said. "We must go in. This will be our first wine tasting." We scurried out of the car eager to sample the fruits of this locale, almost giddy at the prospect. Never mind that it was only eleven o'clock in the morning. The owner, dressed in a worn pair of overalls and a plaid shirt, seemed nonplussed at our entrance. He seemed to find it difficult to get off his wooden barrel of a resting place. It became apparent that tastings were not exactly as we had experienced in our home state of California. No flurry of activity in evidence here. Wines could be sampled, yes, that was possible. But—the man indicated as he finally slid off his barrel and ambled toward us—we were to understand that we were visiting a *co-operativo.* (I am supposing he meant this was no individual winery, therefore, he took no pride in the combined efforts of the vintners whose wine commingled in each bottle.)

Reluctantly he poured a thimbleful of nectar from an open bottle into one paper cup, then tottered back to his resting place. Sharing the sample, we oohed and aahed appropriately. And I tried to remember Italian words of appreciation. *Delizioso* came to mind. Even in a paper cup, the liquid was light, fruity, with a hint of apricot. It was as delectable as Lisa had professed. But the only words I had memorized were "*È una giornata stupenda, no?*" which meant, "It's a wonderful day, no?" Later I realized my error, but for some reason, the man must have sensed our struggle. Or maybe it was the universal sound of my husband's coins hitting the counter, for he slid back off his seat to assist us in the purchase of four bottles of wine.

"For our wine cellar," Win laughed triumphantly, as we headed back out the door.

Before getting into the car, our eyes were drawn back across the river to the looming bluff not far above us. We could see how the buildings had literally been carved out of the earth—the tufa—the porous rock that formed all the surrounding hills. The older, more deteriorated buildings, built on the lowest rim and closest to the river, gave rise and support to the perfectly intact medieval houses built on top of them. All shapes and sizes were capped with rust-colored terra-cotta roofs.

"That is the Longobard Torre," Win said, as he pointed up to the tower which rose above the town. He pulled out a guidebook given to us by Lisa for the surrounding villages, known as the *Hilltop Towns of the Fiora Valley*. He began to skim through the text.

"The Longobard Torre and its battlements are from the 8th century and it looks like the tower has dominated this town since ancient times," Win paraphrased. "The old gateway into town once had a drawbridge and was crowned with a large travertine coat of arms bearing the date of 1545. We'll have to check that out. The inscription is from Gianfrancesco III Orsini, Count of Pitigliano and 'the coat of arms bears witness to the troubled governing of the Aldobrandeschi/Orsini families which ruled the greater part of the Maremma, for well over three centuries.'"

"Hmmm. The Maremma?" Win lifted his head from reading and asked.

"That's the land that stretches from the Tyrrhenian Sea inland through the Tuscan hills," I said. "I'm guessing it was an Etruscan word that referred to land along the sea—*al mare*," I replied. "But the Aldobrandeschi/Orsini families? I'm not familiar with them. The de Medici, yes, The Aldo . . . Orsini, not so much."

"Just keep your eyes peeled, and we'll catch it."

We drove up the road, over the bridge, through the open gateway (crowned with a large, ostentatious bear on the coat of arms) and into the walled city of Pitigliano.

"Gives new meaning to the words 'to bear witness,' wouldn't you say?" I giggled as we passed more examples of the pretentious heraldic coat of arms. (Winston abides my sense of humor.)

Seeing an open parking spot opposite a sign for *formaggio* (cheese) and *salsiccia di cinghiale* (sausages), I pleaded to go into the shop. "While in Pitigliano," Margarita had instructed, "be sure to stop at the sausage shop. They're absolutely marvelous."

Waltzing directly into (literally) any foreign shop is not my husband's forte. But you don't have to ask him more than once when it comes to wild boar sausage. (I suppose we bought too many. I was swayed by my own paranoia that no shops would be open later in the day. Margarita had made an impression on me about the possibility of facing starvation.)

It was nearing noon as we began to wander up the ancient stone-hewn streets and alleyways and around the renaissance fountain at the center of the Piazza della Repubblica. All the museums and shops appeared to still be open. Apprehensively, we attempted to judge when they would close their doors for their lunch hours, their *intervallo del pranzo*. It seemed we were safe at least until one o'clock. We peered over the uppermost walls at the end of the Medici aqueduct and could see the tiny wine shop we had visited less than a half hour before. We continued up, up the narrow gauntlet of streets, where we came upon a castle—a fortress formerly owned by the very *Aldobrandeschi/Orsini* families. Within those *tufa* stones stood a museum of Etruscan artifacts: treasures from an obscure people from the eighth century BC. We were in our glory, as ancient history is one of our many interests and delights. We wandered through the halls of the once regal castle, reveling over the pictures of nearby Etruscan tombs and columbarium. We marveled at the fine examples of copper, bronze, iron, and gold artifacts that had been left behind: hammered bowls and swords, vases, jars, belt buckles, tools, crowns. But we were surprised to find so little basic information pertaining to the origins of these people. Even in the halls dedicated to the founding of this Etruscan city, there were very few hints.

"Although the origin of the Etruscan civilization remains obscure, a recent excavation on the Greek island of Lemnos near Troy has revealed a vast quantity of vessels with inscriptions with the Etruscan or 'Tyrrenic' language which added consider-able weight to the argument that the Etruscan people were of oriental origin," Winston read aloud.

"'Oriental origin?' What's that supposed to mean?" I asked.

"Probably that these people we consider to be from the Middle East were, at that time, known as 'Orientals.' Let me see," Winston juggled yet another guidebook, and read.

"Ancient Etruria lay in central Italy, bounded on the west by the Tyrrhenian Sea (recognized early by the Greeks as belonging to the Tyrrhenoi), on the north by the Arno River (near Florence), and on the east and south by the Tiber River (near Rome)."

"Ah, one of my favorite exotic words—*Etruria*," I said. "That was the magic word Lisa used to lure us to Tuscany, remember?"

He nodded, and sat down on a stone bench within the museum to continue reading: "Evidence suggests that it was the Etruscans who taught the Romans the alphabet and numerals, along with many elements of architecture, art, religion, and dress. The toga was an Etruscan invention, and the Etruscan-style Doric column (rather than the Greek version) became a mainstay of architecture of both the Renaissance and the later Classical revival. The first 'grid system' in city planning began with the Etruscans."

"Amazing," I said.

"So, if they showed up here during the Iron Age," Win postulated, "they were well-established long before the Romans took over. But, their language, which was one of the top three languages in Italy, next to Greek and Latin, didn't survive. Only short passages written for funerary purposes have been found and, according to this guidebook, are still quite difficult to translate."

There was a sudden shuffling movement from the guard as

he began herding us tourists to the front entrance. His lunch hour was clearly upon him, and, it appeared upon the rest of us, if we would only get a move on. We bustled down the well-worn ramp, onto the stone steps, and back down the village streets in search of our own *pranzo,* or lunch. We discovered on that fine fall day, at the Trattoria Il Tufo Allegro, a pasta course with sage—an ancient herb Italians love to celebrate—to be of such a delicate and exquisite flavor that it has now become one of our favorites.

Tuscany

CHAPTER FIVE

Lisa Unwraps Tuscany

*A*fter our leisurely lunch in Pitigliano, we wandered off to the neighboring village of Sorano. As we drove up switchback roads past pine forests and cypress trees, a sign indicated we had arrived at the highest inland point in the Maremma near Mount Elmo. We found Sorano, like Pitigliano, perched atop another vertical tufa ridge overlooking the three rivers.

"I believe I'm beginning to pick up on the dynamics here," I said. "Three deep river gorges can provide a natural defense position. We know Sorano was also well-known for its Etruscan and Roman heritage, but what other treasures did this village have to offer?" I climbed out of the car and began to assemble my walking paraphernalia—backpack, sweater, water bottle, guidebook.

Winston locked the car door. "On the road, we saw signs for the ancient tombs and *columbari*, but let me pull out my trusty guidebook again," he said. He began to read aloud, "The name Sorano is of Latin origin, but was probably derived from a divinity of Etruscan-Faliscan origin."

"Faliscan?" I asked. "Now, what the devil is a Faliscan?" My hand had gotten entangled in my backpack and I was whirling around like a dervish in the parking lot. My husband ignored my antics and kept on reading.

"*'Pater Soranus,* the god associated with mountains and wolves, was the evil counterpart to the Sun divinity, Apollo or Jupiter.' Thus, this town is called *Sorano* and that's that," he concluded.

"So, we're heading into the village of the 'evil counterpart?' What does that have to do with the term *Faliscan?*"

Win tossed an answer over his shoulder, "Not certain, but the Faliscan language was from the now-extinct Italic language of the ancient Falisci. Got that?"

Well, I probably didn't. There was already too much information flowing past me.

We headed out of the parking lot. Immediately upon entering the village, the most daunting history of the town revealed itself in another epoch and another castle. Here was one more medieval drama headed up by, yes, it was the Aldrobrandeschi/ Orsini family—later to be taken over by, my goodness, the Medici family? The same Medici family? I was intrigued.

"Power during the medieval period," Winston reminded me, "had been held solely in the hands of a few ruling families. No city-states to rely on. No big governments." I nodded, as if I remembered that, and trudged up an incline after him. I had a lot to learn. And retain, as well.

The immense fortification, which overwhelmed our senses once we realized the magnitude of it, made the Pitigliano fortress pale in comparison. We opted to take a tour with English thrown into the mix and walked through the medieval monstrosity and absorb the eight hundred years of history that had been played out there.

I tried to imagine the hundreds of years of wars fought outside those massive walls—blood running rampant, boiling oil spilled onto the enemy—yet we were told that never, during any of the sieges, were the walls or draw bridges breached. Through bastions, towers, keeps, cannonball manufacture rooms, and a labyrinth of tunnels we toured. Past one courtyard after another, up multiple sets of stone stairways and ramps, over bridges, on top of ramparts we trundled. Finally, we arrived at the Palazzo Comitale, the residence of the Orsini counts. We were told that Bacchanalian décor, along with frescoes of mythological scenes, once had covered the interior of the residence. We were only to imagine, because the doors were closed and locked.

Opposite the Palazzo was an ancient castle chapel and at the rear of the courtyard stood an elegant triple-arched portico that led back down to the north gateway and to the town below. By then, my brain had begun to fuzz over. So much history to take in, and in just one place. We were exhausted from our day's travel, so we ambled down to a small outdoor *café* where we sipped a luscious cappuccino and gobbled up a couple of crisp *biscotti* for fortification. Yes, we were tourists, and we ordered what we wanted. Then, we headed back to Poderi.

That evening, Lisa and her son, Niccolo, offered to take us out for dinner at a small *trattoria* in Montemerano—again, only five kilometers away. Winton and I leaned into these new friends as if they were lifelines, as we were already suffering from the lack of hearing our own spoken language. I find it always takes immense energy to absorb the verbal and physical cues while visiting a foreign country. Every pore of my body felt stressed from bending forward to capture the essence of what had been said, in a language, with which I had only a nodding acquaintance. Lisa was a sweet respite.

After she helped us order a delectable *primo* course of local pasta, followed by a *secondo* of *Cinghiale al Sugo* (Wild Boar with Tomato Sauce), I asked Lisa what had originally brought her to Italy. I knew she went to Florence to study as a student and fell in love with a Roman. Niccolo, age eighteen, leaned back in his chair. A look of boredom swept his young face, yet his dark Roman eyes, enhanced by the metallic cherry-red hair dye that covered his normally dark-brown hair, never left his mother's face. He was curious about her answer, too.

"Would you also please tell us about the traditions and celebrations you shared with your family in Poderi? Did you celebrate holidays, like Easter, in Italy the same as when you grew up in San Francisco?"

"Well, no, that changed a lot," Lisa said. "Just being in Italy was a major change for me, even before I had my sons. The first Easter I celebrated here was probably one of my most memorable. It was during the year of the flood in Florence. We college students had been in Florence for only a week or two when on November 4, 1966, at six in the morning, flood waters came down the Arno and completely flooded the city. It was devastating for all Florentines. It ended up changing the entire next year for everyone living there, including us. As students, we were enlisted to become part of the relief effort—to go down to help wherever we could, whether in the museums or libraries." Lisa picked up her wine glass, swirled the deep red essence, and took a sip.

"That following Easter there was a wonderful celebration at the Duomo, the Cathedral of Santa Maria del Fiore, called the *Scoppio del Carro.*"

"What was that?" my husband asked her.

Lisa grinned, and put on her teacher's voice. "*Scoppio del Carro* means 'the explosion of the cart.'"

My eyes opened wider. I've heard of strange happenings in churches in our time—explosions, rarely—but never planned ones. Lisa's eyes sparkled as she continued.

"The celebration began the night before, at midnight. Oh, you could hear the bells ring—those great deep bells. If you've heard them chime, you will always remember them." She paused, took a bite of her *contorni* (salad) before going on. "You could hear them ringing all the way up in the valley to the villa where we were staying. It is one of my most amazing memories. The villa was part of the school for Americans I was attending, and it overlooked Florence from the western hills. We were most fortunate to live in such a beautiful setting.

"So, the next day I went down with the maid and a few friends from the villa into Florence. We went into the piazza, which was filled with people, and entered the church to take our seats. The priests were wearing their beautiful purple Easter vestments and the crucifix, too, was swathed in purple satin. A great cross stood in front of the altar and, at an appointed time, a child resolutely walked forward and lit a fuse at the base of that cross. The fuse sent sparks up to the top of the cross which lit another fuse in a small rocket-shaped dove which shot the entire length of the nave and out the front doors of the Duomo and into the piazza. The first time I saw it, I was flabbergasted. I couldn't tell if we were in the 'sanctuary of the holies' or in a circus!" I gasped; she laughed.

"When the dove went zinging out into the piazza," she continued, "it hit the Carro, which is a huge cart—a magnificent, elaborate golden contraption of a thing filled with fireworks—and it exploded! The explosion continued for well over five minutes, echoing in through the nave as people patiently waited for the service to begin.

"This *Scoppio del Carro* ritual, I was told, was handed down from early Christian origins. I think it has some pagan elements too, but I believe it started here in Florence sometime after one of the first Crusades. The spark, or new fire, represents new life once Christ has risen. Thus, this was the celebration of Easter. Now," she leaned conspiratorially across the table to us, "if the fuse was lit and it ignited the little *columbina,* the little dove, and traveled through the nave without a hitch, and into the piazza outside the Duomo, then it was considered an auspicious omen. A good luck charm, so to speak. It was a good thing for the new crops and the beginning of the new year. This was a special tradition in Florence and was such a monumental experience." She sighed as the memory flooded her senses.

"Ingenious," Win said.

Lisa nodded her head and sat in silence for a moment. "Then, after the service, we walked back to the villa where we had a lovely Easter meal with a specialty cake, known as the *Columba cake,* which is baked in the shape of a dove."

"How absolutely lovely. Such marvelous traditions," I said.

"Yes, that's true. It was the first truly memorable Easter of my life. I remember, of course, the gathering of eggs as a child, but this was my first appreciation of Easter being something more. It began my awareness of holidays being something very deep—of being connected to the pagan rituals, the cycle of nature, to God, and to all of humanity. I could see this way of thinking—of living—was intrinsically woven into these people, not as much, perhaps, as wars are, but as an awareness of the connectedness of all life. This concept doesn't come from what we consider as being poor or frugal, uncomfortable, undesirable, or from an inconvenient situation that people have fallen into, due to their ineptness. No. This is the idea of living in a world where gods are everywhere—where your interdependence is on the wellbeing of all of these forces, because for some reason the Mediterranean has this sense of interconnectedness."

She took a deep breath and leaned back into her chair. We quietly closed our mouths, which may have been hanging open. Lisa looked over at her son who was busy doodling on the place mat in front of him. He was still listening to her, though, and nodding his head in agreement.

"That's complex. I really need to think this through," I murmured. "It seems to resonate with the Greek and Roman mythologies we've studied and also incorporates the Roman Catholic faith."

My husband sipped his wine and sat back from the table. "To think that these beliefs—these Mediterranean forces, as you referred to them—are still unfolding three or four thousand years later is quite remarkable, isn't it?"

Lisa looked up from her wine glass and smiled. "Yes, it *is* quite remarkable. And so, that was the first occasion that I remember feeling that there was something special there. And like you said, there had always been something here. It was just my first awareness." She took a few bites more, then put her fork down.

"My experience of life in that villa," she continued, "was wonderful, too, with all the marvelous food. I remember tasting a lasagna there and it was one that I'll never forget. I've tried to replicate it since, but it never comes out tasting as it did in that villa. It was made by Piera, the maid and seamstress. Oh, those Florentines were such remarkable, talented people! She had this wonderful ability to do all these marvelous things. She was part of a fabric of people who learned from observation. You see, there is a certain way to make a lasagna and they—the Italians— know how to do it. And it always comes out with a very specific result. No deviation. That was also my first real imprint of Italy."

I felt as if Lisa was unlocking the keys to understanding of a world I had only just become acquainted with. But I knew the keys she was handing us were precious and this was a rare opportunity, maybe once in a lifetime. I put my glass down and focused more deeply on her words.

"And then I guess after two years, I met my husband-to-be and his extended family. It was within their family I began to understand their great culinary dedication. His mother and her sister were excellent cooks to the point of being severe critics of anyone who would try, for example, to mash a potato in some primitive way. And she would say to her son, 'Now *that* is *not* a mashed potato, dear!' So, you learn that there is an art to things, like making *gnocchi* and other wonderful things she created in the kitchen. But what that hard school of learning taught me by its very rigor, was that there is something enduring about a good recipe—prepared at the right time with the proper ceremony, shall we say.

"For instance, the incredible happenings of the *Scoppio del Carro,* the exploding cart of Easter. Everything has an appropriate time and pattern. Even a simple meal has the same kind of rigorous structure, and that is a lesson that has sustained me throughout my entire adult life."

At that point, a luscious *tiramisu* found its way to our table and we dug in with four forks to savor the decadent sweetness, along with thimble-sized glasses filled with *grappa.* I can't tell you if it was the grappa, the wine, or the loveliness of the evening, but an unconscionable mistake was made as my husband drove us back in our rental car to Poderi.

I'm afraid to tell you it was Lisa who made the mistake. It was done with genuine kindness, but I'm certain she had no way of knowing the demon she would unleash. She made the unforgiveable error of telling my husband—yes, I shudder at the thought even now—that he could drive like an *Italian*. An *Italian?* Gadzooks! Maybe he could drive like Mona Lisa. But Mario Andretti, the Italian American race car driver, he will never be! Sadly, the damage was done. To this day, he prides himself on the glow of her comment. Bless her!

Tuscany

CHAPTER SIX

Etruscan Tombs of Sovana

*T*he following day, my honey and I popped out of bed, excited to get an early start on exploring the Etruscan heritage. That day, we had pledged, we would visit the ancient tombs.

We were so excited at the prospect of climbing into the ancient caverns, even though tales of vipers falling from trees had given us the willies. We were not snake people!

We were soon on the road. The sunlight diffusing softly through the cypress and oak trees, was like spun gold as it rose in dust motes into the air. Winston was clipping merrily along—his driving skills blessed by Lisa the night before—as we headed down the road of San Martino sul Fiora toward Sovana, another village known for a plethora of Etruscan finds.

"Sovana! Sorano! Sovana! Sorano! How do these people keep these names straight?" I babbled on as I tried to find my place in the new guidebook we had picked up the day before in Sorano.

"Ah, here we go. This says, 'The Etruscan area surrounding Sovana has a special importance in respect to other centers of ancient Etruria in that all of the major types of funerary architecture of the Tyrrhenian region are found here.' I wonder what that means? 'The volcanic rock at Sovana was cut, chiseled and worked from the time of the earliest Etruscan settlements in the 8th century BC and their work continued throughout the entire ten centuries of Etruscan history and into the Roman period.' Got that?" I asked. Win nodded his head, but I wasn't sure he had been listening.

"So, where did you say the Etruscan people came from? We got some of this information at the museum yesterday, but I'm still not clear," I said.

"Check in the section on Etruscan Origins," Winston gestured toward the book.

I thumbed my way through to a page called "Origins" and read silently for a few seconds, then began aloud, "Around the fifth century BC, the Greek historian Herodotus stated that some of the Etruscans may have emigrated from Lydia, a region on the western coast of ancient Turkey. It appears there was an 18 year famine in Lydia, so the king dispatched half the population to look for a better life elsewhere. Under the leadership of his son Tyrrhenus, the emigrating Lydians built ships, loaded all the stores they needed, and sailed from Smyrna (now the Turkish port of Izmir) until reaching Umbria in Italy. Of course, this is disputed by Dionysius of Halicarnassus several hundred years later, who believed the Etruscans were indigenous to this area of what is known as Italy."

"But what did he know?" I asked, throwing my hands up in resignation.

"It looks like," Winston said, as he made a U-turn and headed back down another road, "these people, however they arrived, have been here since, say, 900 BC, but no one knows for certain where they came from. Like we learned yesterday, their prolific language is possibly from the island of Lemnos in the Aegean."

"That's right. I do remember," I said. "That's when I was enlightened about the word 'oriental.' You read from the guidebook that 'these people we consider to be from the Middle East were, at that time, known as 'Orientals" Or 'Middle Eastern.' Makes sense to me. Now, do you know anything about funerary architecture?" My husband shook his head but was busy trying to decipher a sign indicating where to park. Again, our Italian was lacking.

"We will be seeing 'chamber tombs, façade tombs, niche tombs,' and also your basic 'burial ditches,'" I read from the book. "And also, rare and magnificent 'temple tombs.' Whoopee! This sounds positively grand," I said, although a bit wary that these were all considered good things. We were talking of death and dying here.

We pulled into the parking lot that indicated the Illdebranda Tombs and stepped out onto a carpet of fallen oak leaves. Even though it was ten o'clock in the morning, ours was the only car in the parking lot. This was not Disneyland, but I had expected some crowds. I can't say the silence was deadly, but it did feel a bit eerie. Last night I had asked both Margarita and Lisa what they thought of these tombs, but in their twenty-five years in Poderi, neither one had ventured over here. And the site was only thirty minutes away.

We put on our backpacks and added water bottles. "All right now," Win asked, "What are we looking for again?"

I could see my earlier narration had fallen on deaf ears—he had been driving—so I turned to the guidebook again. "'You will find at the Illdebranda Tombs, rock-hewn tombs, necropoli, sacred pathways, wells, waterways—all hand cut out of the porous tufa stone. The burial chambers and the Etruscan temple from the Hellenic period of 3rd century BC were also carved with meticulous skill and without the use of mortar or bricks.' Let's take a look."

We were both surprised at the immensity of the beautifully

carved temple. The façade had once rested on twelve fluted Doric columns. Only a few were left standing, but the detail remained indelible. I reached for the guidebook. "'The twelve columns probably alluded to the twelve towns of Etruria, and the capitals, which are now in a nearby museum, were decorated with the four faces of Etruscan divinities, both male and female, surrounded with large acanthus leaves.'"

Win took out his guidebook as well and read. "Etruscan temples were generally square buildings on top of a high stone plinth, with a large colonnaded portico to the front and a cella, or interior chamber, inside. The cella was often divided into three parts in accordance with the Etruscan belief in a triad of deities."

We climbed the steps of "the high stone plinth" to the temple and walked under the once regal canopy of the yellowed tufa portico. We could still make out the concentric squares on the ceiling which, we had read, were representative of typical Etruscan temples. But it was difficult to make out other designs, so I turned to the trusty guide.

"It says, 'The tympanum of the temple—the triangular pediment above the doorway—once had carved floral motifs in a complex mixture of flowers, leaves, bell-shaped flowers, and sacred animals. Along the cornice on the west side, the original sculpted frieze is still visible .'" What? We rushed along to what we thought was the western side to see the details above us. Yes, we could make out a gryphon (a Greek mythological creature—half eagle/half lion), geese, the sun, and other images probably related to the zodiac. The detail was amazing! Outdoors in the elements were images that had been etched into the rock between three to four thousand years ago. We could even make out the original details in the temple that had been plastered and painted in bright yellows and even deep reds. The colors remained.

The morning sun burnished the stones under our feet, as well as turned the air into a sweltering inferno. We hastened down the stairs to go below the temple, where we found two funerary corridors that led us out of the heat but into an almost frigid plane. The main corridor, which was directly below the center of the temple, was a cross-shaped or cruciform burial chamber. It held a long single tufa funerary bed, indicating the temple had been dedicated to an especially important Etruscan. Royalty, of some kind. In the lateral corridors, we found more "beds" that lined the walls for burials of members of the same family. It was difficult to grasp how important this feature must have been a millennia ago. And to imagine how many bodies had lined these walls. Claustrophobia set in.

As we scrambled back out of the tomb, we spotted a sign by the side of the path for the *Via Cava of Poggio Prisca*.

"What is this *cava* we're heading toward?" I asked. "Another cave?"

Looming ahead of us was an enormous passageway, or path, and not a cave at all. It appeared to have been painstakingly carved out of the solid tufa rock. Once again, we checked the guidebook. "Most walls of these Etruscan roads are cut out entirely by hand and are twenty-five meters (75 feet) in height with the path itself being around five hundred meters in length.' Or 1,500 feet long," Winston determined.

He read on. "'The colossal work involved in opening these huge subterranean passages is incredible. High up on the walls are various incisions, often unreadable. Immediately beyond the entrance, high up on the left, Etruscan burial chambers can be seen.'"

We walked forward to see what was visible. Yes, there were small indentations carved into the wall at a great height. He continued reading. "These chambers were lived in by (Christian) hermits during medieval times and during the long and difficult period of Christianization. There are traces of a fresco of the Madonna and Child in a carved niche below." We stood on our tiptoes, trying to keep our balance, as we stared straight up the mossy green sides of the cava.

"They've mentioned the Christian religion, but what about the Etruscan religions?" I asked.

Always at the ready, Win turned to the section on religion and read. "Religion is a major contributor to the aura of mystery which surrounds Etruscan culture. The Etruscans believed in many gods, some of them adopted from the Greeks, and they also believed in malicious spirits: in particular, they worshipped the triad of Tinia, Uni and Menerva."

"Ah, that trinity," I laughed. "Should have known."

Win ignored my snarky comment and continued reading, "The walls of the Cavone are covered in signs and incisions made through the many centuries, including Christian crosses which served to exorcise the ancient pagan gods. In fact, the Cavone was at one time called the 'Devil's Road' and was a source of superstition and fear."

I'm not sure why, but we stepped a little more quickly up the pathway, keeping our eyes moving both up and down, as the pathway was sometimes rutted with deep cuts made from what? Burial carts? This place was so quiet I could easily imagine a funeral procession plodding slowly along the passageway. I had read about the Etruscans' use of human sacrifice and wondered if that would be mentioned. I encouraged my husband to read further.

"Roughly halfway along the passage next to another medieval niche is an Etruscan inscription of the IV-III century BC which reads VERTNE—probably a dedication to the supreme Etruscan god Vertumno or Veltha. Next to this inscription is an ancient swastika, a symbol of the Sun and polarity."

"Swastika?" Win asked.

"Ancient swastika," I said. "The ancient swastika was a symbol used over four thousand years ago. It was Sanskrit and meant 'well-being.'"

We were now at the top of the passageway. We each took a deep breath as, even though unspoken, we felt safe and sound. No mention of human sacrifice yet, but then we still had to retrace the path to retrieve our car. Rats! I opened the guidebook. Sure enough: "A particularly macabre practice (of their religion) was that of human sacrifice to placate the gods and protect themselves from the kind of torment meted out by demons in the underworld which is depicted in their tomb paintings. Victims were forced to kill each other off in gladiatorial duels which took place at funerals." Now, that was an event I would not have cared to witness. *Oh, feet, don't fail me now!* Posthaste, we made a mad dash down the *cavone* or *corridoio* (corridor) and back to our car.

Having spent our morning in the necropolis or "city of the dead," we opted for some living, breathing folks to have lunch with. We drove the short distance through the countryside, over the Fosso della Calesine River and into the village of Sovana, where we parked near the Duomo and found a superb restaurant, La Scilla. We were famished and eager to try everything on the menu, but we chose two wonderful soups: *ricotta zuppa* and *acquacotta.* The first soup was a rich mix of spinach and ricotta cheese; and the second I have made many times since. It is a simple peasant dish that means "boiled water" and is a thick vegetable stew with a lovely poached egg placed on top.

Lisa tells a delightful story about this soup: "This is maybe the most famous dish of the Maremma. It was the poor people's soup, made with a pot of water and any vegetables available. It was regularly taken by the peasants (working for a landlord) to the fields and eaten at midday under an oak tree. Today, there are still isolated oak trees in the middle of fields, even if they are an obstacle for fieldwork. Perhaps you have noticed these trees in the surroundings of Poderi. The soup was cooked in the early morning and kept on the back of the stove or, because it could also be eaten cold, the children took it to their parents during a lunch break or *intervallo del pranzo* at midday. Today, it is a very fashionable dish served in restaurants and, of course, enriched by diverse vegetables."

As an accompaniment, we were introduced to our newest favorite wine, a bottle of Morellino di Scansano Reserva, which was as luscious as the name: a local full-bodied red with lusty hints of morel mushrooms. It was as smooth as velvet sliding over our eager tongues.

Our *secondo piatto* was a "mixed grill" or *grigliata*—skewers of grilled lamb, chicken, and pork. All were succulent and juicy with the woodsy flavors of fresh rosemary and thyme.

Sleepy and feeling the effects of the wine, we decided to drive on to Saturnia to find the infamous *terme*, or hot spring pools, for a refreshing dip. When we finally arrived at the resort, it was already after five o'clock and they had closed their gates for the day. So, we looked for the hot springs that fed the pools, the *Cascate del Gorello*. What we found was somewhat disturbing, as the water was not only hot, but smelly and dirty and there were no showers, changing stalls, or bathrooms. We decided to head back to Poderi and stop off at the Super Marché in Montemerano for a few ingredients for supper, but when we arrived all the market doors were closed. What day was this? So, we headed to Manciano, the larger town on the hill near Poderi, and found—Egad! The same thing! At that point, we were hot, tired, and exasperated. We had so much to learn. Every community is different, but no shop is open after one o'clock on

Wednesdays. Good lord: it *was* Wednesday! We were out of luck as, of course, Poderi has no stores, just a post office, which has its own unusual hours, determined by the whims of the postal officer.

By the time we arrived home, we couldn't remember what we had been so fired up to purchase for the evening's meal, so we ate lightly, bathed, and fell into bed early. Tomb tramping, we found, can really take it out of you!

Tuscany

CHAPTER SEVEN
Firenze (Florence), Here We Come

The following morning we arose early—ah, there is no rest for the wicked, especially those on vacation—but we were heading to Grosseto to catch a train to Pisa, then on to Florence. We had become fond of train rides in Italy, although timetables appeared to be only slight suggestions. Taking the train allowed us to lean back, relax, and frankly not worry if we were "driving like an Italian" or not. As we traveled north to Pisa, the seascape along the Tyrrhenian Sea reflected jeweled tones of aqua blue in the morning light. And the landscape, on our right, was equally beautiful, with medieval castles and villages perched high atop every hillside. Vineyards and fields of sunflowers wreathed around the village, lazily soaking up the autumnal morning air.

Three hours later, we pulled into the Florence train station—at the Santa Maria Novella Station—with our list of Florentine places to discover: The famous Duomo, Campanile, Uffizi Gallery, Piazza della Signoria, Ponte Vecchio, and the Arno River, to start. We were eager to find the homes of Renaissance writers such as Dante, Petrarch, and Machiavelli plus view some of the works of Florentine artists such as Michelangelo, Donatello, and Botticelli.

As I've mentioned earlier, our Stanford classics professor

considered Florence to be the true center of the universe, if not the "navel" of all cultural enlightenment. He was biased because he had taught there for thirteen years, but we had come to Florence to find out for ourselves.

We found Florence a most frenetic city. People of all nationalities flooded out of the adjoining train cars, into the station and onto the sidewalks and narrow alleyways. Noisy *motorinos* (motor scooters) were as common as the housefly as they screamed through the streets at breakneck speed. Taxi drivers used horns instead of brakes. The air was a faint blue from exhaust, yet the aroma of savory grilled sausages and marinara sauces beat out the competition for our senses.

I slowed our progress through the streets. I stopped to drool before the beautiful *pasticceria* (pastry shop) windows featuring pyramids of *dolci* (sweets) which were piled high in colorful arrays. Buttery tarts bursting with custard-cream fillings such as *gianduja* (chocolate and hazelnut) or chocolate with orange zest, which called out suggestively. An *il fornaio* (bakery) also competed for my attention with savory aromas of pizzas-by-the-pound or *pan di rosmarino* (glazed rolls filled with raisins and rosemary). Winston cajoled me to continue to our hotel first, but I took note to return later.

It had been awhile since breakfast and I felt as if I was starving as we dragged our suitcases down the cobbled streets to our hotel. The brochure in my sweaty hands said the hotel was only "300 feet from the steps of the S. M. Novella Train Station." Perhaps they meant meters. Ah, well. To complicate matters, the sidewalks and streets were vastly uneven, and we hefted our luggage up and down and over every curb for blocks before reaching the hotel.

The Atlantic Palace Hotel, "part of an antique palace which dates to the 1600s but originally an old monastery," described our new home for the next three days. Our room was spacious, clean, albeit spartan—probably a throwback to the monastery days. We dropped our bags in the room and raced out to grab a quick slice of pizza or panini. No leisurely lunch for us today, as Lisa's dear friend, Cecilia, was due to pick us up within the hour. A resident of Florence, she had kindly offered to be our tour guide for the afternoon.

Cecilia arrived at the appointed time with her darling ten-year-old daughter, Camilla, who raced into the hotel to escort us out to the awaiting car. Before we had spent even an hour in Florence, we were whisked out of the hub and the bub—in fact, out of the city altogether—and began weaving through the olive orchards and climbing into the foothills to the north. Cecilia was taking us to a famous ancient Etruscan/Roman village known as Fiesole. Like a jeweled crown, this seventh century BC village sat atop a cliff that overlooked the entire Florentine valley.

Again, we were drawn into the past as Cecilia and Camilla graciously guided us through an archeological site that included an Etruscan temple dedicated to Minerva, a first century BC Roman amphitheater, baths, and lap pools; and the Museo Faesulanum, a museum featuring collections of ceramics, funerary art, and metal works from the Bronze Age through Byzantine times.

I was almost giddy with excitement, and Winston was ecstatic. Our years of studies were finally paying off and to be able to share our excitement with someone who also knew and loved this history was truly a gift. To see my husband drooling over these discoveries in almost the same way I had been reacting earlier to food brought joy to my heart.

One of the most extraordinary and colorful exhibits at the Basilica of Sant'Alessandro was the Della Robbia ceramics. This was a representation of religious glazed sculptures from the rebirth of terracotta sculpture and continuing throughout the Florentine Renaissance (1400–1525) created by generations of the famous Della Robbia family. What extraordinary artwork and exquisite craftsmanship.

"I can't believe we're actually seeing these beauties up close," I whispered to Winston. "They are even more vibrant and beautiful than we saw in our classes about the Della Robbias."

"Everything is more colorful," he murmured. He was in awe.

"*Magnifico, si?*" Cecilia intoned. Her greenish eyes sparkled with delight.

Speaking of beauty, I took another look at darling Cecilia. She was a gem, giving up her day to take us on tour. Were we lucky or what? No wonder Winston was enjoying himself. He was surrounded with Florentine splendor.

After an hour or so, we wandered out the front door of the Basilica and across the street to find ourselves at a viewing area that overlooked the entire Arno River Valley and Florence far below us. Mellow golden evening light shimmered off the heated city only a few miles away. Rising proudly from the light was the red terra-cotta dome—Brunelleschi's dome on the Duomo. *Domani! Tomorrow! We will see it tomorrow.* It's been written that Florentines can't begin their day without being within sight of this great dome. (I had been reading *The Agony and the Ecstasy: A Biographical Novel of Michelangelo* by Irving Stone, and these thoughts came to mind.) Just then a breeze glanced off the surrounding hills and cooled us. We clambered down the steep hill into the center of Fiesole and headed for a local trattoria Cecilia recommended. We four were famished.

Miraculously, we were able to get a great table outside under the grapevine-covered pergola. The evening was comfortably warm, and we enjoyed a magical night of laughter, good food, and wine with these new friends. The rich, autumnal pasta with porcini mushrooms was delightful as our pasta course, but the *fritto misto* took center stage with light batter-fried local vegetables, along with chunks of rabbit, chicken, and beef. Thank goodness, the portions were small.

Speaking of center stage, we had been marveling at the impeccable service we were receiving that evening, along with a steady flow of wines, when it came to light that Cecilia, a former model, was now an actress in Florentine productions. We should have known, as she had attracted a bevy of waiters who continually hovered nearby. (No wonder we so easily secured a good table. She was famous!) She had never given us a clue beforehand.

Around midnight, Cecilia dropped us back at the hotel in Florence, where we collapsed into our beds, totally exhausted, but serenely happy.

The following morning, we rolled out of bed too late for breakfast and we were mildly reprimanded by the staff for our tardiness. This must have been a throwback to monastery life, though that seemed overstretching it a bit. Our agenda was full anyway, so we grabbed a pastry and a double-espresso and tossed back the ink black liquid as if we knew what we were doing. (I didn't! Cough! Choke! Cough!)

Then we zipped down one of the alleys to the Lorenzo de' Medici Chapel. Again, I was using *The Agony and the Ecstasy* as my guidebook, and this was the beginning of our tour, as the chapel housed Michelangelo's gift of sculptures to his patron, Lorenzo de' Medici. San Lorenzo, the parish church of the Medici family, was where Lorenzo the Magnificent was buried. Although Michelangelo never finished the project, sculpture of the "Medici Madonna" was Michelangelo's own work. The sculpture of the Madonna holding the baby Jesus was beyond magnificent and four times life size.

Next, we fended our way through the throngs to the Duomo. Impressive at any angle, this incredible building and campanile are ensconced in green, white, and pink Tuscan marble. The orange-tiled dome, which we had seen from Fiesole the day before, was difficult to see from street level due to the long cavern of buildings surrounding the church. We toured the Duomo and found ourselves staring at the painting, *Dante Explaining the Divine Comedy,* by Michelino. (No, not Michelangelo.)

Although Dante (1265-1321) grew up only a few streets away, the Duomo was under constant construction during his lifetime and the dome was not completed until well after his death. But his life's work continues to influence the world of Florence and beyond. We made our way to the front of the sanctuary where the high altar stood. I found myself searching for the wires to the *Scoppio del Carro,* the lines Lisa had told us about which, on Easter, would carry the flying dove through the church and out the main door, to hit a cart and explode. Laughter enveloped us both and we were forced to leave. (One, or in this case, two, can only handle so much glowering of docents.) We would have to return at Easter to catch this spectacular event.

Outside, we rounded the corner and headed to the Uffizi Gallery. We began to laugh, as there, just like Cecilia had told us there would be, was a line of hopeful museumgoers that snaked along and around the inner courtyard of the museum.

"Thank you, Cecilia," Winston whispered to the wind. "Amen!" I responded. Cecilia had taught us the trick of purchasing our tickets at the train station before arriving at the museum in order to miss the long two-hour wait in line.

"She just saved us a whole lot of afternoon," I said, as we

strode to the front of the line, handed over our tickets, and, yes, sanctimoniously waltzed in.

The Uffizi, known by many as Italy's greatest art gallery, houses some of the world's finest Italian Renaissance works—those of Botticelli, Caravaggio, Giotto, Titian, Piero della Francesca, Raphael, da Vinci, and of course, Michelangelo. Collected over many years by the Medici family, some pieces come from many points throughout Europe. We found it curious that most of the artistic themes were religious in nature. Our English-speaking guide explained: "Wealthy patrons paid artists extremely well and in addition gave them extensive periods of time to complete their work. This was a wealthy man's way of buying passage into heaven!"

"If that's the case, we have very little hope," I mumbled to Winston. But we were grateful to those who hopefully had made it (to heaven) as well as provided the world with the best artistic expression from the twelfth century to the sixteenth century that Italy—or the world, for that matter—had to offer.

We lunched on the roof of the Uffizi overlooking the Piazza della Signoria and surveyed the mosaic rooftops around us. Excellent tile work was visible only to those who had climbed to our vantage point. After lunch, we strolled down to the riverfront of the Arno and made a left-hand turn into the Institute and Museum of the History of Science (now Museo Galileo). Winston became ecstatic! He had ambled through the Uffizi just fine, but now all cogs in his scientific mind came to life.

The museum houses the collection of scientific inventions collected by the Medicis during the fifteenth and sixteenth centuries. We saw Galileo's actual telescopic lens—the one through which he was able to spot four moons of Jupiter. (Have you ever seen a grown man jump for joy, like I saw my husband jump?) We saw golden astrolabes, telescopes of all sizes and shapes, maps, globes, and a most amazing astronomers' armillary sphere, which filled an entire gallery and showed Earth as the center of the universe. (Yes, this was an enormous issue for the Church, with science constantly pushing hard against the issues of faith and religion.)

Each room was filled with inventions from varying scientific disciplines including astronomy, cartography, plus the first instruments to measure time and navigation. For a sailor like my husband, the museum became a home away from home. And even though I haven't the same scientific bent, I found the exhibits fascinating. Can you imagine seeing the very first compass? The very first medical tools? Every invention has a beginning, and many beginnings were exhibited right here.

After a couple of hours or more, we made our way along the Arno River to cross the famous Ponte Vecchio. This, the oldest surviving bridge, was built in 1345, but was a replacement of the former Roman bridges that crossed these waters. Indeed, this was the same river Lisa had spoken of when she described the damaging floods of 1966.

The bridge originally was built with a gallery which stretched its full length with blacksmith shops, butcher shops and tanneries, but was later replaced with high-end gold and jewelry shops. Those shops still exist today. We made our way back and forth through the crowd and eventually returned to the Piazza della Signoria.

We found an open table on the Piazza and had a much-needed cappuccino. Above us, dark foreboding clouds were rolling in from the Tyrrhenian Sea and were beginning to boil as they moved east toward the mountains. All forms of mankind flowed past us—more monks and nuns than I'd seen in my lifetime, and I had attended a Catholic women's college.

"Makes me wonder what Rome will be like," I said to Win.

He nodded, but kept looking around us, as there was much to see. So much had happened right where we were seated.

We were loving Firenze; the history, the art, the majesty of the place, and knowing that such prominent writers, thinkers, and artists had made their way here—right here—to blossom before and during the Renaissance. It was simply extraordinary. I could almost feel the history surrounding me.

"This was right where Lorenzo de Medici's dream came true —for Firenze, and for men like Michelangelo," Win exclaimed.

"And over there was where Savonarola, the religious leader, tried to bring the Medicis down!" I said. We had learned of the Dominican priest Girolamo Savonarola in our classics' classes. He was the one who took it into his control to burn objects that the church authorities considered sinful, such as cosmetics, mirrors, books, and art. This was against everything the Medicis revered, back in the late fifteenth century. And Savonrola wasn't going to allow it!

"Ah, yes, that was the Bonfire of the Vanities," Win said, "and for his efforts, he ended up being burned at the stake right there in this very square too—Piazza della Signoria."

A replica sculpture of Michelangelo's *David*, along with Neptune's Fountain, stood directly across from us. And in the adjoining Loggia di Lanzi, an enclosed but outdoor porch, the famous and dramatic sculpture by Giambologna, *Rape of the Sabine Women*, which stood along with ancient Roman statuary of former emperors.

"I wonder how many people know the real story of this rape?" I asked Winston. "Was this sculpture created as an acknowledgement of the atrocities by Roman men? Or was it wrapped up in mythology to cover up their crimes?"

"Ah, the tug and pull of life through history," Win said, wisely. He reached across the table, grabbed my hand, and led me back to the hotel for a much-needed nap. The cappuccino, which I'd sipped as a pick-me-up, somehow hadn't done the trick.

That evening we made our way across the street from our hotel to a recommended and lively restaurant, Ristorante Le Fonticine. Named after the sixteenth century Luca della Robbia fountain outside the front door—yes, the same della Robbias we became acquainted with during yesterday's foray to Fiesole. We found the restaurant pleasant and friendly—and what can I say—it looked like a typical Italian restaurant with artwork and murals covering the walls, and the tables were covered in—yes—red and white checked tablecloths. The aroma of fire-grilled meats whetted our overactive appetites, and we ordered deep red Tuscan wine to accompany our meal. That night we sampled two local pastas: *Tagliatelle al proscuitto e punta di asparagi* (egg noodles with prosciutto and asparagus) and the house pasta, *Taglierini Fonticine,* noodles made with another luscious mushroom and truffle sauce. We shared the *Bistecca alla Fiorentina,* a two-inch thick Porterhouse cut of beef, grilled rare over coals. A must for all steak lovers, and certainly when in Florence. And for dessert we had fresh berries with, as the menu indicated, another local specialty: sweetened mascarpone. (Are you getting hungry yet? Thought so!)

Throughout the evening, we were entertained by the banter of the staff and chatted with a couple from Dublin, Ireland seated next to us. They were celebrating their 25th anniversary and one bottle of wine turned into two or . . . So, that night when the staff offered their *digestivo* of grappa, they also offered *limoncello.*

"Well, how can I say no to lemon transcendence in a thimble-sized glass?" I trilled to the Dubliners.

But, dear reader, how can I warn you that after sipping this potent lemonade, you, too, will never be the same? If there was ever a recipe I wanted to get my hands on, this was the one. But as the staff told us: "Beware! Be within crawling distance of your bed because it can hit you fast."

Blithely, albeit glassy-eyed, we crawled back across the street to the hotel and directly into bed.

The next morning, we awakened to a soggy, wet city. We had put off any video coverage previously, so then we were forced to slog our way back through the city streets retracing our steps to the Duomo, past the de Palazzo Medici, the Uffizi Gallery and back to the Arno River in the rain. We were absolutely drenched, so we did what we *always* do—when seeing an umbrella concession, we bought a new one. (We now have a collection of twenty-five umbrellas, none of which ever seems to be at hand when needed.)

Having captured the city by video in a deluge, we rushed back to the hotel to pack and head to the train station for our noontime train. Our time in beautiful, albeit wet, Florence, had come to an end. Saddened to leave so soon, we looked forward to our return, hopefully soon.

CHAPTER EIGHT
Wet and Wild at Terme di Saturnia

*W*hile traveling in a foreign country, have you ever collapsed into bed at night totally exhausted because you spent the day leaning forward to catch the nuances of a translation? (Oh, I know I've mentioned this before and probably will again.) Sometimes that works; sometimes, not so much. As we left Florence, the *mistranslation* was about trains and train schedules. We hopped onto a train, which we thought would go straight through to Grosseto with the accoutrements of a dining car. Instead, it was a "slow" train without even the whiff of stale coffee. Instead of a quick three-hour trip (of which we paid for) this train took its own sweet time getting us back to Grosseto— four to five hours later than expected.

Pisa, only forty or so kilometers away, or twenty-five miles from Florence, took well over an hour. In fact, we arrived in Pisa three times—going back and forth, back, and forth—something to do with getting on the right track—and we had yet to see the actual Leaning Tower. And Pisa was not even our final destination.

At least, we told ourselves, we were traveling in the right direction, skirting once again south along the Tyrrhenian Sea. The waves thrashed wildly against the shoreline below the train, but the rain had stopped, and the day was becoming warm, even hot. And, we were hungry. No, we were famished! We had eaten little breakfast and it was already turning three o'clock. Rats!

At one point, when we had pulled into yet another small village station—perhaps the twentieth village station along the route, we waited for what seemed like an interminable length of time to continue movement. I finally lowered the window and poked my head out. The train car was stifling and humid. I needed a breath of fresh air. As I stood there steeped in my own sweat, I heard the voice of a young man calling out, "*Panini! Panini!*"

My eyes grew large. I thrust the window open wider and leaned out over the tracks. I waved my arms wildly at the young man. *"Panini! Panini,"* I echoed. My husband stared at me, astounded. I turned, grinned at him, and grabbed my purse. I was so excited!

There are singular moments of ecstasy while traveling abroad, when you understand what is being said. The boy was selling *panini*—sandwiches—pressed hot salami and cheese sandwiches, as it turned out—and we were saved. Starvation abated.

"I don't think I've ever been so proud of you," Win said, as he licked the last of the cheese off his fingers. It was an experience too short-lived, but never mind, we got our *pranzo*. Little triumphs like this can carry you for years!

After another hour, we were finally able to pick up our rental car in Grosseto. We drove leisurely down the coast a few miles and stopped at Porte St. Stephano for a late afternoon cappuccino. (Yes, we do love our cappuccinos!) Always attracted to the sea, we sat at a small seaside table watching as a ferry loaded passengers to head across to Isolde Giglio. (Little did we know at that time that this tiny island would become famous for the tragic sinking of the Italian cruise ship, the Costa Concordia, in 2012).

We headed through the hills to Poderi where Lisa came to invite us to a community dinner—the last of the food from the *festa.* But we were exhausted and opted out. We probably should have gone, but the tiny cells in my brain had ceased to accept any more strain from languages I didn't know. *"Domani! Domani!"* I said. "Tomorrow! Tomorrow!"

We awakened on Sunday morning to church bells ringing and overcast skies. We had been on the road for ten days, but it seemed like it had been weeks. It was definitely time to wash some clothes. Another hurdle to leap in a foreign country is to figure out the appliances at hand. Some washers work on a principle of centrifugal force—forwards, then backwards, then forwards again—taking well over an hour for each cycle. Because Lisa's washer was not known to us, Lisa came bounding over to give us a hand and help us conquer our ignorance.

"Dryers? No, thank you. We don't have one," she said, with a quick repartee.

So, we learned the trick of hanging out of the second-story bedroom window, where the clothesline was attached to the house and a tree in the backyard. Precariously, we took turns dangling our wet ensembles along the clothesline pulley system—pulling and leaning, leaning and pulling—until every article had been artistically displayed. Just as we placed the last clothespin into place, a crack of lightning and a roar of thunder sent us hurtling back inside. I slammed the window shut. The heavens opened, and a second rinse cycle ensued.

"I guess we could have put soap in the pockets, then hung them on the line," Win laughed. Ah, well! (I love my pragmatist husband!)

Just then Lisa came back in the front door and asked if we would like to go with her to the *terme* in Saturnia. "It will be raining off and on today," she said, "but since it's a hot water spring, we will be in water anyway. So why not?" We agreed, ignoring the earlier crack of lightning. Why not? So we headed off for our adventure hoping to find our clothes still on the line and not strewn across the valley when we returned.

"Saturnia got its name from the Roman god, Saturnus," Lisa said, as she drove through the hills and valleys on the way. "One legend has it that Saturnus grew tired of the constant wars between humans and sent a thunderbolt to earth which created a magic spring of hot sulfurous waters, which over time came to ease the pain of mankind."

"Sounds like it would be good if *all* mankind came for a long soak," I said, watching the landscape blur past us.

"How hot is the water?" Win asked. He, too, was eyeing the gray clouds and drizzle that seemed to be following us.

"The temperature is said to hold at 37. 2 degrees Celsius, or around 99 degrees Fahrenheit. It's quite relaxing."

Hearing those words, Winston settled back in his seat and did just that. Relaxed. "Perfect temperature for us, I'm sure!" he sighed.

At the spa we made our way into the modern facilities that housed the bathhouse, showers, and snack bar. These grounds were massive, and the facilities were part of a luxury hotel/spa with four pools and various smaller pools and showers. I figured we could spend hours traveling back and forth between all the options, but we began in the larger pool connected to the hotel. The water, a deep mossy green color, made the bottom indiscernible. The pool was cordoned into swimming lanes with white floats holding ropes in place. We eased slowly into the pool. Why slowly? The water was hot, and because everyone else was moving in slow motion. No diving, no fast swimming; no one was even swimming laps. In fact, folks were dangling on the ropes to keep their heads above the water or were hanging on the sides of the pool doing the same. The water was steamy hot, and all our energy dissipated. Greenish-black globs of moss, or some mysterious substance that had floated up from the bottom of the pool, hovered around us. (No, I didn't go down to check it out).

"I know it looks disgusting," Lisa said, "but the moss is supposed to be good for your skin. You're supposed to rub it on your face and body. This is a beauty treatment that has been practiced here for possibly three thousand years."

Three thousand years? "Okay," I agreed. But first I looked around to see how others were handling this "treatment." They seemed as disgusted as I was, but I decided to give it a short go. First, I paddled farther out. I didn't want to make a spectacle of myself so close to the side of the pool. And then while hanging onto a rope, I attempted my "facial." I figured it couldn't hurt. I scooped up a handful of moss and began to pat it onto my cheeks. I looked around, but saw no others as foolish, so I scooted the muck down to my arms instead and rubbed it around before piling on more. Before long I felt I must look like the Monster from the Black Lagoon, so I dipped under the murky waters to rinse myself clean. It worked. *At least, I tried it,* I thought. I paddled back to the side of the pool, relieved that all gunky remnants had glided off. *Thank goodness.* But now my eyes were burning from sulfur. In fact, it was difficult to see the side of the pool and, for some reason, the smell of rotten eggs became even more pronounced. I hit the side coughing and sputtering.

Winston, already out of the pool, reached down to pull me out. "Let's try some other pools!" Again, I was game. But once I hoisted myself up, I heard the titter of children's laughter around me. Win, coming to the rescue, began to pluck one, then two, then half-a-dozen globs of green gunk from my hair, my ears, off my suit and from my cleavage. I had failed to rinse the stuff off. Because I had gone blind and couldn't see a thing, I had made a spectacle of myself after all. Well, I was grateful that only Lisa and Winston knew me.

Some of the other pools were long and shallow, just knee high, and could be used to strengthen the legs by walking back and forth. Others featured benches where we could sit with warm water showering over us. Some were like Jacuzzi tubs with massage action, while others were waterfalls made up of large rocks with water cascading over us. It was all glorious and we tried each one. We even opted for a hot panini in the snack bar. This time we only had to huddle out of the rain in order to eat.

But the strangest thing for me was the bathroom, *il bagno*. The fully modern facility had no modern toilets as we know them. Instead, there were only holes in the floor with slick ceramic tiles in the shape of footprints on either side to indicate where to place your feet—and in which direction. But the ceramic tiles sloped down toward a twelve-inch hole. With slippery wet feet, it was all I could do not to slide right on in. (I had nightmares about that later.)

But all in all, the terme was a wonderland of options. By the time we reached home, we were fully relaxed. We laid a fire in the fireplace and spent the rest of the afternoon reading, sleeping, and simply resting. Oh, and rescuing our clothes off the line to dry in front of the fire.

Because of Lisa's friendship with the owners of the restaurant, Passaparola, in Montemerano, she was able to secure reservations for dinner that evening. I was thrilled. I had read of this very restaurant in the book, *Under the Tuscan Sun* by Frances Mayes; it was one of the author's favorite restaurants in the whole Etruscan area. That evening we were to dine in that exact place. We arrived precisely at 8 p.m., as good restaurants don't open before that. (Don't expect them to. It's just not done!) In the entourage for this grand occasion were several of Lisa's friends, as well as her son, Niccolo. There was Margarita, her sister Charlotte from Switzerland, and a visiting couple from Austria—eight in all.

Lisa greeted the owner and his wife and spent a bit of time catching up before introducing us all. She then graciously presented them with an extra copy of the book *Under the Tuscan Sun* we had brought on the trip. She stood by the fireplace, translating aloud the parts that mentioned them. They politely smiled, accepted our applause, then gratefully placed the book on the mantle in the dining room. It was a grand gesture and we felt proud to be honoring them—even though they had never heard of the book, the author, and spoke no English. Ah, well, language barriers are made up of moments like these. I guess we hope for the best, shrug, and adjust our expectations.

The restaurant was lovely, the owners warm and charming, the food delectable. We began with a variety of bruschetta which we shared up and down the table. Then, we had *aquacotta*, that wonderful thick, rich *zuppa* (soup) that I love with a poached egg nestled on top. This was followed by a *secondo piatto*, which for Win was roast lamb and for me stuffed zucchini blossoms. But the piéce de résistance was dessert: tiramisu! *Delizioso!* On a scale of one to ten, this was an absolute twelve. The best we'd ever tasted, and we usually make a point of tasting them all. Lisa called the owner over to the table for us to express our great pleasure and with another bow and a flourish he made quite the show of presenting us with the house specialty, tall frothy cappuccinos. (Who said Italians don't have cappuccinos at night?) They were superb, as were all the local wines we had gratefully consumed. We eased out of our seats at midnight and with Lisa (fortunately) at the wheel, we floated back through the moonlight to our "home" in Poderi.

CHAPTER NINE

The Psychololgy of Place

So, Lisa," I asked as I placed *antipasto* of melon and prosciutto before her, "how are Italian families different from our own families in the States?" Lisa, Winston, and I had spent the next day—Monday—leisurely walking around the town of Poderi, down to the post office, through the hillsides of harvested grapes, and back home. To continue our conversation, we invited Lisa for dinner that evening, and I had tried my hand at cooking *Italiano.*

"Excellent question," she said in her school-teacher fashion, "as your question goes to the heart of all of their traditions—their Italian traditions! As I mentioned the other night, this is a detail—this understanding of the traditions—is what we all need to really pay attention to, or we will miss it." She picked up her glass, swirled the rosy liquid in slow motion, then set it down again without drinking.

"Perhaps I noticed the differences in this Italian culture for the first time when I was a student, and then again as the young wife of a Roman. But I found it's there when you are present in those moments . . ." She paused. "And it's not there when . . . well, it's difficult to describe."

"Sounds like you are about to tell us the secret of the universe and everything in it," Win said with a grin, quoting from one of his many favorite authors, Douglas Adams. He stuffed his napkin into his shirt collar and smoothed it down over his chest.

I, too, felt Lisa was leading us toward something important—something so meaningful, and I hoped I could grasp the depth. I sat down at the table beside her, and we waited as she sorted through her thoughts.

"Well, it's not all that serious," she grinned, "but let me back up. There is a very precise schedule to things in Italy, and everyone observes that schedule—even the Parliament stops at one o'clock and they go off to lunch and enjoy a full *primo* and *secondo*—nothing more, nothing less. It's something about order, I think. It's sort of a classical thing. Here in Italy people have a precise schedule within their lives that determines when they do things. And it's not just a daily schedule, but a yearly schedule, too. For instance, you eat only seasonal vegetables during that season. No other time. And you are, of course, doing this with all your family. So, when I say there is a rigor to it, it's through their schedule—it's a kind of grid of things and everything fits into that grid. It's not the Anglo-Saxon way of handling things—that's for certain!"

"What exactly do you mean?" I was eager to understand.

"For instance, in the States, you are always rushing to get somewhere, then you go through the motion of doing what you came to do, then you relax! Aaah! But then you rush to do the next thing, just to get through it, and it is all so stressful! Do you understand what I mean?"

Win and I nodded our heads. Yes, we understood. We were worn to the nubbin from doing just that at home, and that was why we had raced to Tuscany for our vacation. She had nailed our American cultural model to the wall. I walked into the kitchen to get the evening's *primi piatti*, or pasta course. As I filled a platter with *tagliarellini* and splashed boar sausage marinara over the pasta, I thought about what Lisa had just told us. There are rare times in our lives when we realize, in the moment, that we are about to be given great wisdom. I felt this was one of those moments. I needed to focus my thoughts.

I placed the platter in the center of the table next to a block of Parmigiano-Reggiano cheese and laid a small grater to the side.

"Help yourself," I said. "This is how we Americans do things."

Lisa smiled kindly and swirled a modicum of noodles onto her plate. We leaned in closer, waiting for her to say more. Out of the corner of my eye I realized our elbows were now resting almost in the marinara sauce which had begun oozing down the side of the platter and onto the table. I tried to ignore it.

"Why does this stress not exist in the Mediterranean?" she asked us. We blinked but had no answers.

She continued "There is something about *flow* in the Mediterranean that is always present. It is characteristic of the people and I must say, in a guarded kind of judgment, I think it really *is* the Mediterranean people." Her fingers thumped against the table as she contemplated this further.

"Perhaps it's the geo-psychological origins from a long, long time ago—from the Phoenicians or from the Etruscans. All people from around the Mediterranean are one. They have a shared culture—like a . . . like a psychology of place."

Geo-psychological origins? The terms rolled through my thoughts as I tried to make sense of them. *Is there a psychology of place? Is that what she means?* I had only a small inkling of what this might convey, but I was eager to learn.

"So, you're saying the so-called grid or 'schedule' that was culturally set up here eons ago is what sets everything into its place now?" I asked. She nodded.

"So, is it like a characteristic that some geographic places have, and some do not? Or a feeling or perception people hold?" I asked her again.

"Yes. It might be the Mediterranean people's connection to the solar part of them—the sun and the seasons. Or it might be the sea part of them—the tides, the ebb and flow that connects them to the Earth."

"Ah, now that must be the answer," Win, the sailor, said with a confident air. He sat back in his seat as if all pieces of this mental puzzle had ebbed and flowed into a comfortable mooring.

Lisa smiled kindly. "Yes, I'm thinking that might be part of the answer. It's all very powerful, and without words it roots each person, each Mediterranean being, to what is, and to what is good."

"Are you including the Etruscans in this mode of thinking?" I asked.

"Yes, the Etruscans had a lot to do with this way of thinking. I think the Etruscans were a great source of *carpe diem*. You know—seize the day and life is good? They went about selling and trading olive oil and wines all along the Tyrrhenian Sea— from the Côte d'Azur in southern France, and all the way back down the Tyrrhenian Sea along the peninsula that would much later become Italy, and as far east as Turkey. Their commerce was good. The Etruscans were not conquerors, mind you; they had no interest in conquering people. You probably learned some of that while you were visiting their tombs and museums, right?"

"Now that you mention it," Win said, as he twirled a forkful of *tagliarellini* around in his plate, "I think we learned their culture was riveted in structure, just like you said. In fact, they were the first to set up grid systems in city planning and . . ."

"And their rituals," I interrupted, "were structured around their values and beliefs surrounding the cycle of life and death—or the after-life. Much like the Egyptians, the Greeks, and the—"

"Exactly," Lisa said, "and they all came from around the Mediterranean. But then the Romans moved in—as Romans are wont to do." She smiled, having been married to one for over twenty years. "And the Romans learned from the Etruscans, absorbed all their best ideas, then took over. The Etruscans didn't put up much resistance and were quickly overcome. And that is another part of the Tuscan culture—those who were indigenous to and connected to the natural world did not fight."

"So, you discovered all of this when you came here to live?" I asked.

"Yes. I found these people have a strong allegiance to their village first, then to their region—even though Italy has been a formalized country since the 1860s."

"I heard there is something called *campanilismo,* which refers to the love of the campanile or tower of one's home village. Is that what you mean?" Win asked.

"Exactly! Exactly!"

"Now, we spent several days last week learning about the powerful families who ran the countryside, like the Aldobrandeschis, the Orsinis, and the Medicis. That was before the city states or regions came into being, right?" Win asked again.

"Right! But, as you experienced at the festa here in Poderi, people still have an affinity to their own regional cultures, traditions, dialects, and foods. That is what defines who they are."

"That was the best time, Lisa," Win said, stuffing more pasta into his mouth.

"Yes, the experience of a lifetime," I echoed. "We can't thank you enough for encouraging us to visit this time of year." We were obviously still in the glow of the festival. "But, continue on."

"I remember once," Lisa said, changing the subject, as she twirled her fork into her pasta, "in a restaurant in either Bologna or Modena, when I asked for tomato sauce on the tortellini. The waiter looked at me with disdain. 'Signora,' he said, 'we don't ever put tomato sauce on *this* dish. But I will bring you some sauce on the side.' I realized that I had made a terrible mistake—an absolute transgression. Sometimes I would make a dish in a traditional way and serve it to my Italian friends, and they would say, 'This is not *Tortelli di Bolognese*,' simply because it was not made in a very precise and particular way.

"When I was first married and cooking in Poderi, I would prepare food for our neighbors in what I thought was the traditional way. And they would say, 'Oh, no thank you.' I'd say, 'No thank you? But this is what's for dinner!' They'd say, 'No thank you, I don't eat that!' I knew my food was prepared somewhat according to the recipe, but I guess it was not *exactly* right. So they were reluctant to eat my food. This always seemed strange to me. I didn't realize people could dislike foods in such a very strong way—just because it was not prepared *exactly* the way they were used to eating it. Or how their grandmother had prepared it!"

Win and I looked at each other with surprise. "I had no idea," I said. "How could anyone pass muster here if they were born on the outside? However did you manage?"

Lisa smiled. "I certainly learned a lot while living here," she said.

I looked again at the concoction I had boldly prepared with boar sausage and a marinara sauce which was now beginning to congeal on our plates. Lisa threw her head back and laughed.

Obviously, she recognized my momentary feelings of inadequacy. She picked up a slice of bread, dipped it into the small bowl of rosemary-scented olive oil I had placed on the table, and popped it into her mouth. I took note of my plate of cooled pasta and swirled up a nest of *tagliarellini* and stuffed it into my mouth. I'm not proud. I'm hungry!

"Once," she continued, "when my son Sasha was seven, he brought another child home for lunch one day, and I served him a plate of pasta with tomato sauce on it. The child looked at his plate with horror and disbelief and asked, 'What is this green stuff in the sauce?'

"I said, 'That's chard from my garden.'

"He said, 'Oh no, I could *never* eat that. I can't eat pasta that way.'

"I thought about this for almost a year, and finally I realized that these kids in Poderi wouldn't eat *anything* unless it was in the same recognizable form they were used to eating. They will just choose to go hungry instead."

Shock must have registered on both our faces because Lisa burst out laughing. "Yes, it was a shock for me, too. Oh, and let me tell you, these kids won't even eat a birthday cake if it's not the traditional, regional, recognizable birthday cake they know and love. One year for one of my boys' birthdays, I prepared a *torta montalbana corte crema*. I tried grapefruit icing only once— the kids looked at me aghast and wouldn't eat any of it. I realized that you just don't break rules. Even for seven-year-olds, you just don't break the rules."

We laughed again in disbelief. "That's so hard to imagine," I said. "I'm trying to place that into a context back in the States, and I'm drawing a blank. Usually, the parents win out by making the child 'try something new' or demand they eat everything set before them."

"I struggled with it too," Lisa said. "But I found that I could use children as my greatest teachers. From their school and from their family environments, the children learn that things are done a certain way, and that there is only one way. Once I adapted to this theory, I found it was true. My organism—my body—now needs in the evening a certain thing such as *pasta in brodo* or *crema e verdura* because it is good at that time of day. You also need a siesta in the heat of an afternoon. And when you are sick, there is certain ways to eat, called *in bianco*, which means to eat only bland things. I found it profoundly comforting to know this science of living."

The three of us sat back and quickly tucked into the remnants of the *primi*, then I headed into the kitchen to pull our *secondo piatto*, or *pollo al sale* (chicken encrusted in salt), from the oven. We thoroughly enjoyed the chicken—it was so succulent and juicy even I was surprised. (Thank goodness I wasn't cooking for a full-fledged Italian, though.) As Win refilled our glasses with wine, Lisa continued our discussion.

"So, this attitude—this way of being—became woven into my life as I was raising my children. I learned the ways that women connect with their culture through the use of food and I, too, became skillful in my adapting to these different experiences of one's family life."

"Are you referring also to the way certain foods are part of certain holidays or celebrations? Like at the festa?" I asked.

"Yes, exactly! For instance, you have all these wonderful things at *Carnivale*—capricious, delightful cakes, plus the sweets and seasonal cakes that take up to three days to rise. Oh, it's all so beautiful—this whole process. Once I tried to make one of these cakes with the people in Montemerano. At that time, they had a bakery—a forno—where you could bring your cookies in to be baked for your child's communion. Because you would be serving eighty people, you would take in sixteen trays of cookies in the morning. And they would bake them on a low heat in that wonderful wood oven. Then, you would pick them up in the afternoon. It was also possible to take in a small cake, or these great trays of cakes or cookies."

"Sixteen trays of cookies? Who on earth has sixteen trays to bake cookies in the first place?" I asked. (I'm thinking logistics, here.)

"The community," she said with a wave of her hand. "Oh, and this was such an interesting thing, too. Everyone had to make exactly the same thing, and in exactly the same way. I mean it. Every mother made exactly the same meringues, for instance."

She leaned forward as if again whispering a secret. "I was able to use that oven to bake our things, too, including my whole wheat bread and whole wheat cookies. I'm certain the neighbors found these items to be questionable at best!" She sat up and smiled. "But, honestly, it was not a sense of trying to offend anyone or of being capricious or spoiled. No, no, no.

"When the little seven-year-old refused to eat my chard-enhanced pasta sauce, he simply said, '*No grazie.*' I didn't think children would feel they had the right to say that to an adult. But there it was; it was just, '*No grazie.*' 'Do you want something else?' I asked. '*No grazie! Bene cosi!*' This meant, 'I am satisfied.' I think at that point I finally realized that food was a profoundly serious business. It is meaningful. Almost spiritual. They don't eat between meals. They just don't do it! And if and when they do, the food has to be exactly like what their mother or grandmother makes."

"I'm so amazed!" I said. "I think of our five kids and grandkids as being picky eaters—one doesn't eat red meat, another eats only red meat. One eats only vegetables, and one won't eat anything with cheese or milk products. And I had another who only ate foods that came out of a window and in a Styrofoam box. And I consider myself a decent cook!"

"Yes, she is," Win said.

"But an entire culture eating only what their mother puts before them?" I exclaimed. "It's astounding!"

"Hmmm," Win said, with a twinkle in his eye. "What would they think of your little sign in the kitchen? It says, "'Today's menu: take it or leave it.'"

Lisa nodded and grinned. "They would probably handle it better than our American children. That's for sure. Here in Italy at ten o'clock in the morning at school, the children take a break and have *merènda,* or a mid-morning snack. There is a wonderful story about a little boy in Sasha's second grade class, who came to school on the bus from the country. When the break rolled around, this kid brought out a great big lunch box. Inside was his napkin to wrap around his neck, a little tablecloth, plus his plate and spoon for the pasta. He was all set to have a nice warm meal. The kids watched with disbelief. He had his whole house all set up there. 'That's a nice lunch you have there, Roberto,' they said to him. In this case, his family had sent him off to school with his whole *ethos*—his whole extension of home and family—all wrapped up in that little box.

"Of course, that didn't last long, I'm sure. Normally, the kids brought just a sandwich—a little *schiacciata,* which is Tuscan flat bread stuffed with a bit of prosciutto, for their break. The little ones would all go home at one o'clock for their warm lunch; the middle-schoolers would go home at two. That meant none of them ate at school. They just went to school from eight o'clock to ten o'clock, had a little break, and then continued until one or two o'clock in the afternoon. Then, when they went home for their hot lunch, they needed to have specific things. If it was a cold day, they had polenta with mushrooms. If it was a medium-cold day, then it was gnocchi with tomato sauce. It was simply understood that when the bus pulled up in front of your house, the pasta would be *al dente*, steaming hot in a dish, and awaiting them. Sometimes I found that was a challenge, but that's what all the mothers would do. In the beginning I felt this to be oppressive at times, but I learned quickly it was a way of living and structuring your life, and that an enduring pleasure comes from that type of structure. Actually," Lisa leaned toward us and said in a conspiratorial voice, "I found it was quite restorative—a very wonderful thing."

"What about for single adults? What did they do?" I asked her.

"If you didn't have children and a husband coming in from work, then it was not quite as rigorous. But friends of mine, who didn't have that kind of structure, still observed the propriety of time and the kinds of foods they cooked, because that was part and parcel of the whole fabric of their lives. I learned that was and is the way you do things in Italy. And it was and is a sustaining thing! You get great strength in that."

As I'd been listening to Lisa, I bit into a chunk of bread, the aromatic tang of the rosemary-scented olive oil nipping at my taste buds. I had also been envisioning a society—the Italian society—that seemed to me to have a stranglehold on individuals' lives. Was it just me, or did others feel the same? My hand self-consciously moved to my throat and I began to choke.

"It sounds like a whole lot of rigidity in the way families 'do' food," I sputtered into my napkin. Tears blurred my vision, so I couldn't see Lisa's reaction to me, but she placed her hand over mine and patted it.

"Are you all right?" she asked kindly. I nodded. I didn't say so, but I couldn't imagine tolerating the confinement of spirit.

No wonder I felt like I was choking. I promised myself to remain open-minded. At the same time, I was remembering that nowhere in Italy had I been served butter or olive oil with my bread. Never! It was never done—and now I was beginning to understand why. What I was sputtering over was only an American thing. And probably my understanding of my own ethos.

CHAPTER TEN

La Dolce Vita – Parc Nationale de Maremma

*O*n our last full day in Tuscany, Winston and I headed out early for the coast of the Tyrrhenian Sea. We wended our way back down through the hills on that bright, clear morning heading toward the ancient Etruscan seaport of Talemone. The city, perched within Sienese fortress walls, sat precariously on a sheer cliff jutting into the sea.

"According to an ancient mythological legend handed down through classical Greek literature," I read aloud from my guidebook, "the original village was called Talamone, named after Talamone, the banished son of King Eacus of Aegina. Supposedly, this village was established along the Tyrrhenian Sea when Talamone sailed with Jason of the Argonauts in search of the Golden Fleece. They were on their return to Colchis."

"That's odd. They must not have had a GPS or maps like ours," Win said, "as *Colchide* or *Cholchis* is somewhere off the Black Sea near Russia." He had read a very old version of the story of Jason and the Argonauts

"That can't have been easy. Flying must have been involved. They were gods, right?" I giggled.

Win shrugged, and I continued perusing the guidebook, "Supposedly, Talamone, this great Greek hero, also fought in the

Trojan War, died here in Talamone, and was buried under the promontory. Hmmm. We'll have to check that out. Ah, it also says that archeologists found fragments of Etruscan sculptures dating back to before 150 BC."

I read more: "The terra cotta panels found depicted the final deed in the cursing of Oedipus in the myth of the *Seven versus Thebes*. This was a subject with which the Etruscans identified the end of their own history in this area."

"That's an odd observation," Win said. "I wonder how they knew it was the end of their era and how does that explain the Sienese walls? We're not close to Siena."

I shrugged. "Good question. This article says the Etruscans lived in this area from the eleventh century BC until the first century BC, so maybe they saw the writing on the wall—so to speak." I grinned. Winston grimaced.

We pulled up to the base of the town and parked in the lot next to the sea wall. We contemplated the steep climb up the hill into the walled city of Talamone. Something clicked—was it a sign? I can't recall, but we were suddenly brought up short. It was once again a Monday, and we realized the tourist office would be closed—as well as the museums and most of all *i bagni*, public bathrooms. Rats!

(By the way, we had found, by this point on our trip, that we could navigate the Italian language fairly well—as long as we knew two phrases: *Dové il bagno?* (Where is the bathroom?) and *Il conto, per favore.* (The check if you please.) It was amazing how many miles (or kilometers) we were able to travel with these two tidbits of language.)

We walked along the sea wall staring up at the fifteenth century Sienese fortress above us. Barricaded against the marauding hordes throughout time, this one town had moved from Etruscan to Roman to Sienese to Spanish occupation.

Yes, so many stories were harbored here, but we would have to catch them another day. We fortunately had come to the sea for a beach day, so we popped back into the car and headed north to Alberese and the Parc Nationale de Maremma in search of the perfect place for a picnic along the water.

The National Park stretched from inland hills, through the Uccellina Mountains, over swampy land, through sand dunes and down to marinas or onto sandy beachheads. Silvery-green Mediterranean *maquis* (shrubs) and olive trees were scattered throughout the landscape with regal oak, maple and lovely umbrella-shaped pine trees guarding the primitive dusty roads we bumped along. Patches of myrtle, lavender, broom, and rosemary scented the air and whetted our appetites. For our picnic we stopped at a small food truck that carried our favorite short-order food: Panini. We bought a couple of sandwiches, some potato chips, oddly named 'Teenagers,' and some drinks, and hopped back into the car.

The normally turquoise blue of the sea had turned muddy brown from the past couple days of storms. So, as we ventured along in search of the perfect picnic spot, we found little beach left. It appeared the sea had taken massive bites out of the sandy cliffs, leaving scrub oaks clinging to the few spaces, and leaving only a few narrow points of access to the sea. No matter. It was a gorgeous, warm, crystalline day and we soaked up the sun on the only patch of sand and beach we found. We became caked with grit and grime from head to toe as we shimmied down the sandy cliffs to poke our toes into the murky waters before clamoring up again. The sea continued its turbulent foray, back and forth, back and forth, but we made the best of our *piccolo picnic,* or tiny picnic.

After finishing our cheese and sausage paninis, I began knocking the chunks of sand off my feet and started to slip my shoes back on. All the while, I was instructing my husband to be certain to check his shoes for scorpions. Just as I stood up, I realized I had strapped my shoes on with some little creature trapped between my toes. We both panicked—the creature and I! With great trepidation I ripped off my shoe and threw it. Out staggered a much-bewildered beetle who scurried quickly into the underbrush. Gasp! Fortunately, this was one beetle I didn't mind sharing my shoe with, but I'm certain he had other thoughts in mind. Then, to find my shoe. Thankfully, I had thrown it on shore.

After two hours of sun and fun, we headed down the coast to another of two ancient Etruscan/Roman seaports—Orbetello and Porte' Ercole (Port of Hercules). It was 4:30 p.m. and *everything* was buttoned up tight. No cappuccino shops—nothing—so we headed back home. We were hot, dirty, tired, and ready to begin cooking our final Tuscan supper in our little abode. But when we hiked up the hill from the car park in Poderi di Montemerano, we were greeted by Margarita, who popped out of her house to invite us over for a farewell dinner. How sweet was this? How could we resist? What lovely friends they all had become. We carted all our best leftovers to share—wine, cheeses, sausages—with Margarita, her sister, Charlotte, and Lisa, all present to help celebrate our final hours in Tuscany.

The evening began with sherry, followed by a gourmet feast prepared by Charlotte: savory rosemary-roasted potatoes, plus an eggplant and tomato bake, only to be followed by her succulent veal marsala. The evening was filled, as always, with plenty of conversation, laughter, and wine. Then Margarita brought out some of the last nibbles from her famous seventy-two egg dessert. Originally prepared for the festa, she had frozen the remaining wedges.) To this lovely custard torte, made with cream and eggs, she had added some fresh fruits and red food coloring drizzled from the bottle over the top. "A very old recipe, indeed," she said.

As our eyelids were beginning to droop, Charlotte appeared with coffee and her own homemade limoncello. Homemade? We had hit the mother lode! After sampling the best limoncello we had now ever tasted, I persuaded Charlotte to relinquish the recipe. She confessed that she often brought the necessary grain alcohol with her in a water bottle when she flew from her home in Switzerland to Italy. (Those were the good ole days—when we were still allowed to bring a water bottle on a plane.)

We stumbled out the door and back across the street lighted only by a hint of moonlight. Floating over the cobblestones with our accustomed afterglow, we obviously had had a blush too much wine again. But this time, with the awareness we had spent our final night—a very special night—in Tuscany with good friends, good food, and the promise of more days and nights in Tuscany whenever we returned.

CHAPTER ELEVEN

The Amalfi Coast – Getting to Know Amalfi

*T*he day we left Tuscany, we headed out of Poderi around six-thirty in the morning to catch a nine o'clock train from Grosseto. Our journey would take us south through Rome, past Pompeii, near Naples, and on to Salerno in the Campania Region. From there, we would catch a bus up the Amalfi Coast. The train was late—or we were extra early—and we tried to remain patient. But how many espressos can one drink in a morning and sit still?

Finally, pulling out of Grosseto at 1 p.m., we headed south along the Tyrrhenian Coast, which by that point had become a comfortable companion. But this time we were finally seeing new territory and were excited that we'd see some of Rome. The landscape of the high hills to the east began falling away into gentle, sloping plains, while the crystalline sea to the west drew our attention. But the sun's caustic reflection on the water forced us away from the windows, and we stumbled down the darkened aisle to the dining car. Ah, what a novel idea. We lunched on pizza Margherita, which was not bad at all. It was a light lunch, but with a glass of wine, we found it a complete relief to be seated in a dining car at all. We had expected nothing more than a little round man pushing a small cart with biscotti and a whiff of strong espresso. Memories of me screeching through the open train window for a quick panini had yet to fade, but we could see life was improving.

We flew past kilometers of Roman aqueducts awaiting our first glimpse of the great city. Just as we made entry, those same blasted ancient walls ended up blocking our entire view of Rome. We saw nothing. *Niente.* Caught only a peek of part of Rome that could have been left unseen. That's train travel for you. *Non c'è problèma!* Our appetites were whetted for a Roman excursion for our return trip. As they say, all roads lead to Rome, and we knew we would be back in a couple of weeks.

We arrived in Salerno around five o'clock and were told the last bus up the Amalfi Coast was due to leave shortly. We scurried out of the train station at Piazza Vittorio Veneto, and while I waited with the luggage, Win rushed off into the streets to search for the bus station. Unfortunately, we had received erroneous information at the train station, and spent twenty minutes frantically looking for a specific *tabaccheria* (tobacco shop) where we had been told to purchase tickets. Finally, he found the bus terminal and together we raced, with all our heavy bags rattling and banging on the cobblestone streets, to catch the last bus of the day.

Dripping with perspiration, plus exhausted from the anxiety of our full-court press dash, we collapsed into two empty seats. Noticing we were tourists (how could she tell?), a sweet Amalfitan woman encouraged us to move to the opposite side of the bus where we'd have a view of the sea. *"Tutto il mare! Tutto il mare!"* she kept saying as she swept the air with her hand. Yes, indeed, we could see all the sea—the entire Gulf of Salerno, which skirts along the south of the Amalfi Peninsula. We had been told this route was one of the most beautiful drives in the world. We thanked her repeatedly as we changed seats.

Along the beautiful, but very steep, jagged coastline skirting the Gulf, the bus raced up route SS163 with the driver constantly beeping his horn. "An interesting system of driving," we whispered to each other. "Typical of Italian drivers," we smiled. "Such a noisy horn," we quietly concurred. Shaking our heads at the bus driver's folly, we sat back and tried to ignore the blaring ruckus. But we came to realize that the bus driver was warning oncoming cars of our approach. In that way, he rarely needed to slow down for any of the more than one hundred sharp curves we careened around on our ascent up the highway.

On one particularly tight bend, our bus came nose-to-nose, or bumper-to-bumper, with another tour bus. We gasped. Others squealed! Before either bus could back up or move, a small *motorino* (motor scooter) chose that exact second to zip between the two busses' bumpers, before fleeing up the hill.

Slipping down in his seat, Winston gulped. "Under no circumstances would the thought to pass at that moment ever creep into my mind," he said. "Nothing, no nothing in my DNA would have . . ." He patted his sweaty forehead with his handkerchief. We chose not to face forward to watch the road any longer. Instead, we turned to look at the sea.

The sun was beginning to slip behind the mountains as it cast its last golden rays across the azure waters. We sat back to enjoy the incredible panorama. The view had expanded tenfold, as we had by now risen to an altitude of more than one thousand feet above the water. I looked down. Straight down the sheer precipice. There was nothing remaining between us, the road, and the sea. *Tutti di mare?* All the sea? Egad! That was an understatement! As gullible tourists, had we just been tricked?

At just about this point of the trip, a ticket agent made his way down the aisle, collecting tickets. "Interesting concept. I've never seen this on a bus before," I whispered. "Most efficient,"

Win quipped. When the agent arrived at our row, my husband confidently handed over our much sought-after, much sweated-over tickets. The agent took one look at them and immediately became excited. He was speaking right at us—and rapidly at that—with his voice rising in volume with every syllable. *"Questi biglietti non sono convalidati! Questi biglietti non sono convalidati!"*

"What is he saying?" I asked Win. He shrugged, but it was clear that we had broken some preordained rule. And this was no small matter. Suddenly, I was aware the entire group of bus patrons had swiveled in their seats to gawk at the *Americano* imbeciles in question. *Mi dio!*

Apparently, we should have had our tickets validated (punched) prior to boarding the bus, but we had no knowledge of this bus etiquette and had felt darn lucky to have gotten on the bus at all. With great distain, the agent grabbed our tickets from Win's hand and stormed to the front of the bus. Our future lay in his clenched fists, as he waved his arms wildly explaining our transgression to the bus driver, who, rather fortunately, did not also turn in our direction as he drove.

"Are they going to make us get off?" I asked. My face was red with embarrassment. Win shrugged. We slid deeper into our seats while the verdict was being decided. Eventually the agent returned, waved our now-mutilated tickets in our faces, and continued down the aisle to the back. Since the driver didn't stop to kick us off, we decided the bus driver, obviously, had a bowl of pasta awaiting his arrival at home and didn't want to delay our trip—or his—any further. We breathed a momentary sigh of relief.

The bus continued onward for over an hour more, passing through one medieval village after another. We began to cover our eyes as we careened around each curve, where each town appeared to cling over the side of the rocks to which they were anchored. The drive was breathtaking, beautiful, frightening, and awesome. With our hearts in our throats and the trepidation of being thrown off the bus still cloying at our edges, we fell in love with the Amalfi Coast. Yes, this was one of the most beautiful, albeit frightening, drives we had ever experienced.

Alas, we arrived in Amalfi much after dark. The bus park, located along the harbor of Amalfi, was on the lowest edges of town. To reach our accommodations at the appropriately named Hotel Amalfi, we took a taxi up the steep, winding main street to the center of town. After simply dumping us out of the car at the Piazza Duomo, the driver extracted our luggage from the trunk and set it boldly on the street beside us. He pointed his short stubby finger at a set of steps, which wound steeply up, up the streets—known as ancient alleyways. He waved us on with a brief *"Buonanotte"* and *"buona fortuna."* Good night and good luck!

Well, we were grateful for the rest we had received on the bus trip—as traumatic as it had been—so, we girded our loins for the trek up the stairs, dragging, banging, and bumping our bags after us. And, finally, there we were—at our hotel at the top of a thousand steps, just like we had read in the brochure. And, just as the brochure had described, the hotel was "right off the main piazza, Piazza Duomo." Sort of. We swore that on our next trip, we would pack more sensibly.

Our hotel room was large, with space for four. It seemed luxurious, but we were told, "Don't get too comfortable, because we are giving you this room for only one night." The receptionist cleared his throat, bent his head down, and continued. "More modest accommodations will be provided elsewhere in the hotel for your remaining three nights."

Okay, we can live with that, we surmised. Our room was clean, and the shower could accommodate three or more of our closest friends. But we preferred only the two of us at that moment. It had been a long day and we needed to wash off a day's worth of odors from train, bus, and racing through the streets, before we could lumber up more stairs for dinner.

We found out meals came with our rooms, which was a nice surprise. We also discovered we were surrounded by tour groups of elderly Brits. No worries. At least we could relax knowing the dining room wait staff would understand our language.

The evening meal tended to be substantial, but bland. Now, that was disappointing! "We could have gone to my boyhood home in New England for this," Win grumbled. "My mother and grandmother used to boil the meat and vegetables, pour off the flavor, and then serve them for dinner."

We tittered at his memories and bought a bottle of bold red wine. We didn't care where we were that night, as we had weathered the train ride, the bus ride from hell—which had scared the bejeebers out of us—and found our way into the enchanted village of Amalfi. We looked forward to the morning light to check out our surroundings. And to experience the cuisine of southern Italy where the food was known to be transcendent. Succulent, even. Ah, *si, domani, domani!* Tomorrow!

After a night of howling cats and barking dogs, we awoke slowly. Throwing open the draperies, we discovered our window opened above a lovely little garden which, surprisingly, revealed people's front doors, their open windows, and their lives—only a few short meters away. We found we were in a city which was tight on space (and had been for a couple of millennia), and we realized our lives had ceased to be independent from anyone else's. We were all breathing in the same air, weren't we? Giggling kids racing down the steps, arguments taking place in kitchens within an arm's length, all seemed to be taking place in our bedroom. Of course, we didn't understand a word anyone was saying, but somehow it wasn't an inconvenience, but a joy. We were enjoying life's universal banter.

After a continental breakfast, we met with the hotel concierge to set up tours for the next three days: a boat tour to Capri, a bus tour to Pompeii, and a walking tour of Amalfi that would start in an hour. We then headed into the streets (or alleys) of Amalfi. Most streets were so narrow two people could not walk side by side. Why, a small woman with two large shopping bags of food could not have passed through. What was the reasoning for this architectural maze? We hoped to discover that on our historical tour.

We zipped back down the many steps that led to the Piazza Duomo and the heart of Amalfi. By now the sun was dazzling as it launched over the extraordinary rise of monumental cliffs 4,300 feet above us before dropping down into the narrow Mulini Valley and spilling onto the Duomo. The stunning black and white cathedral, the Duomo of Saint Andrew, rose sixty-two steps above the Piazza and appeared to be a riot of stripes, arches, and mosaics with architectural touches gifted to Amalfi from obvious conquering influences: the Moors, the Byzantines, and the Normans. Oh, plus with a splash of Baroque! Sunlight glanced off the green and yellow Moorish majolica tiles that covered the adjacent *campanile* (bell tower). I couldn't wait to hear about the history, but, again, would have to wait for our guide.

Making our way through the Piazza, we discovered fruit stalls offering a profusion of ripe purple plums, dark figs, and enormous peaches, plus garlands of garlic, and string upon string of bright firecracker-red dried peppers. We gasped at the size of the bright yellow lemons—definitely as large as grapefruits. And then, we discovered (joy of joys) boutique after boutique filled with shelves of glistening golden goodness called, *sfusato amalfitano,* or better known as Amalfi's world-famous limoncello. Bottles of all shapes and sizes, filled with both creamy and clear liquids, called suggestively from the shop windows. We smacked our lips. We salivated.

And, in direct competition, ceramic shops flirted with tourists, revealing the same colorful and artistic influences of the Duomo—Arab, Byzantine, and Baroque—but, on gorgeous hand-painted plates, platters, vases, olive oil cruets, and more. Stationery stores, or *cartolaio,* proffered arrays of thick, hand-made paper known as *bambagina,* which we found to be another Amalfitan specialty.

Heading down the main street, we spotted a small nautical gift shop. In no time at all, we purchased an early birthday gift for my sailor husband. It was a beautifully crafted barometer made right in Amalfi, but, surprisingly, the barometric pressure and other small details were written in French, like *beau* (beautiful) or *pluie* (rain).

We then wended our way out of the city gates, past the bus park, and up close and personal to the port. When we arrived the night before, we hadn't realized how close Amalfi was to the water. In the morning light, the beauty of the bay was breathtaking—a crescent-shaped beachhead sheltered by sheer cliffs that were capped with pastel-splashed villas, hotels, terraced lemon groves, and olive orchards.

Shading my eyes, I peered across the water to the southwest, where our hotel concierge had said we would be able to make out some islands in the distance. "Could one of them be the island of Capri?" Just whispering the word "Capri" evoked images of Roman decadence and luxury unsurpassed.

And, just like magic, the answer arrived. High-speed catamarans landed, loaded up with tourists, and disappeared like water spiders across the crystalline sea. Yes, we, too, would be heading to Capri. The day after tomorrow!

CHAPTER TWELVE
When Michel Speaks, We Take Note

*H*earing a call, we whirled around and saw a short, swarthy, and kindly-looking man waving to us from twenty feet away. No more than five feet tall, this barrel-chested man stood with a small circle of tourists about him. Wearing plain white shorts and a flowing white shirt that nicely covered his girth, he also sported a matching crocheted white beanie. This topped his abundant black hair and was conveniently tied into a bun at the back of his head.

Again, he waved, gesturing for us to join him. This was Michelangelo, our morning tour guide, and we obviously looked the part of the American tourists he was seeking to fill his tour. We made our way to his side and became part of a group of twelve English-speakers and voyeurs of history.

Once Michelangelo gathered us together, he rolled up his sleeves and had us turn to face the sea. In his deeply resonant, yet soft voice, Michel—I will call him Michel for short—began to fill our heads with the stories of Amalfi, beginning with some of the most "ancient of mariners," as he called them.

"You may have heard that according to the myth, Hercules built the city of Amalfi on the very spot where he buried his beloved sea nymph, *Melphe*." He pointed to a spot on the shoreline near where we stood along the Bay of Amalfi, to the place of this mythological burial. My eyes snapped open. Michel smiled. "The sea nymph's name was pronounced '*mal-fee*,' which eventually morphed into '*a-mal-fee*,' as you can see." Again, he smiled.

"Most likely, Amalfi was settled by the Romans who lost their way or were shipwrecked on their journey to Constantinople in the fourth century AD, escaping another barbarian attack on Rome. But I think people populated this place long before.

But how far back?" Michel said, as he tossed his hands into the air, "I have no idea; and that's all I got!"

"Well, now," I said, "that was the shortest, most succinct tour I've ever been on. Thank you very mu— "

"No, no, Signora," he said, as a deep laugh, which began at his knees, erupted from within him in an explosion. "No, we are just getting started! Now, follow me as I fill your heads with maritime history."

Winston was becoming as excited as a little boy on a rainy day with a new pair of boots. Have I mentioned before, sailing is his passion and the history of sailing and sailors has become an obsession? With imaginary galoshes on, he marched in lockstep directly behind Michel as we all trundled behind in great anticipation. Standing with our toes almost tippling into the surf, our guide led us back through time, beginning with his description of Amalfi being the first of the Maritime Republics of Italy.

"As I mentioned to you before, little was known about Amalfi until after the fourth century. It was with the pursuit of the Crusades that Amalfi became a powerful trading partner with the Byzantines. In fact, the town of Amalfi was the capital of the Maritime Republic, known as the Duchy of Amalfi, an important trading power between 839 and 1200 A.D. As one of the first Italian maritime republics in the ninth century, it rivaled Pisa, Genoa, Venice, and Gaeta which is just fifty miles north of Naples on the coast," he said, with a wave of his right hand, "as a naval power in trade with the East (Eastern Mediterranean). It was only through trade that the rest of the world came to know and acknowledge Amalfi." Michel turned around and had us face the town of Amalfi.

"Isn't this exciting?" I whispered to Winston. He shushed me just in time.

"Over there," Michel pointed, "you will find the ancient arsenal, which is documented to have been built in 1059. The term 'arsenal' comes from the Arabic term '*Arsina*' as the first arsenals were supposedly built in Northern Africa in 698. All you must do is look around here in Amalfi, and you become a witness to the rich influences of the Arabic people. Now, what are the arsenals for, you ask?" We nodded our heads, and I expected an accounting of all the weaponry that had been stored.

"The arsenal was constructed for the purpose of building the many ships used by the merchants for trading all over the known world. Some say it was for warships, but many of the ships were strictly for trade."

Winston gasped, and I realized from his expression that he was ecstatic at learning this history. Only four or five generations ago, members of my husband's family had worked as ship builders: whale ship builders in New Bedford, Massachusetts. I tuned back into the middle of Michel's discourse.

". . . shipbuilding became an important part of commercial development for Amalfi and drew to her shores many artisans, woodworkers, and sailmakers, who then became permanent residents of the city. Their personal needs helped develop Amalfi because more artisans and merchants arrived to provide shops, markets, provisions, cobblers, house builders. And, of course, more merchants of all kinds who wanted to trade with the world arrived here needing ships."

"Who did the Amalfi people trade with?" one man asked.

"A very good question! We have evidence that they traded with almost all countries surrounding the Mediterranean. During the sixth century, Amalfi began trading grain and timber with its neighbors, slaves from the interior of Italy, and salt from Sardinia, all in exchange for the coveted gold dinars minted in Egypt and Syria.

"Of course, this was in order to purchase and trade Byzantine silks from Constantinople. It is said that the grain-bearing Amalfi traders were welcomed into the Islamic ports and earned the distinction of being able to trade in both Islamic and Christian ports. Because of its prowess on the seas and influence in international trade, the *Tabula Amalfitana*, or Amalfi tables, which they created, provided a maritime code that was widely adopted by all maritime powers throughout the Mediterranean. In fact, merchants of Amalfi were using gold coins to purchase land in the ninth century, while most of Italy was still working in a barter economy."

I could feel Win quiver with delight at all this maritime information we were hearing. It was like a gold mine to him.

"At one time, the arsenal," Michel continued, "which was made up of galleys—cross-vaulted rooms built of local stone and supported by repeating pointed arches—had up to twenty-two pillars to take care of the multiple aspects of shipbuilding. But now it is limited to two rooms, due to the damage sustained many years ago. One room, for instance, was for the preparation of tar, which was used as a sealant on the bottom of the hulls."

"Can we go inside?" Win asked.

"It might be worth your time, but the building is in bad shape. A new museum is supposed to open in a few years with examples of the row-barges used in the Historical Regatta, some architectural and sculptural remains, and several models of ships, as well as a venue for visual art exhibits. Not sure when that will open, though."

"So, what happened to it? How long was it used?" another tourist asked.

"All good questions," Michel replied. "Even Petrarch, mentioned in his *Epistole Familiari*, mentioned the terrible seaquake of 1343, which devastated this town and swept away much of the arsenal."

"Seaquake?" a tall gentleman to my side asked. "What was that?"

"I'm glad you asked," Michel said, as he led us farther along the waterfront. We were playing right into his hands. "There are several explanations, which might be helpful. Today, we would consider it a tsunami. But, in that time, no force of nature from the sea had been experienced or recorded in quite that same way. It was said that Amalfi was being invaded by pirates, which was a common occurrence back then. At that time, a relic from the Duomo of great St. Andrew, himself, was brought down to the sea and held up over the waters. This was to discourage the invasion that was about to take place. At that moment, the seas backed away from the beaches—due to the power of St. Andrew, of course—and in so doing, the waters swallowed up the pirates." We gasped, but he continued speaking.

"Immediately upon witnessing the pirates' demise, the people fled into the hills. They had never experienced a 'miracle' like this, and they feared the pirates might return. So, as it turns out, many were spared once the sea rolled back onto land, sweeping up the shores and into the city itself because the people were in the hills. The fact that the Duomo was only slightly damaged made those remaining souls repent of their sins and never question the will of God. As you will see, the power of myths and Christianity have a strong influence on all Amalfitans."

We proceeded across the street to the center of a round-about. Michel stopped before a unique sculpture—one of a life-sized man riding atop a pure white wave with a pool of water at the base.

"Before we leave the waterfront, I must explain to you that one of the famous Amalfitans is this gentleman, Flavio Gioia. It is said that even though the water compass had been discovered centuries before in China, Gioia is credited with inventing the first dry compass, which is known as the 'mariner's compass.' In the western world, this was the compass most used by seafarers."

Again, Winston beamed and nodded his head appreciatively. He knew that even with all the newest technology for today's mariners, the compass was still one of the most reliable.

Our guide then began to herd us past the buses along the Lungomare dei Cavalieri, through a throng of cars where we dodged and wove between *motorinos*, then we skittered quickly across the Via Matteo Camera into the ancient entryway of Amalfi. Yes, we were making our way up the same streets we had just wandered down, but now, with Michel pointing out the historical aspects of each place we encountered, we were seeing it as if for the first time. Plus, his introductions to many of the local characters along the way deepened our appreciation.

"When we walk through the upper streets and alleys as they are called, you'll notice that no one street is straight, but winds up and up as if it has a mind of its own. Since pirates had invaded this city on numerous occasions, Amalfi was constructed with the intent of confounding anyone who tried to come ashore and take advantage. If you can picture in your mind the construction of a pinecone, you will envision the layout of these streets. All for the purpose of muddling through the thousand years of ma-rauding hordes.

"More about Amalfi. Despite the devastating setbacks, such

as the 'seaquake', she had a population of some seventy thousand reaching a peak about the turn of the millennium. Then in 1073, the Republic fell to the Normans, but was granted many rights. Again, due to the Crusades and during their return home to northern France, the Normans took over southern Italy; Sicily in particular, and used it as one of their principal posts. Amalfi was added to their conquests." He stopped for us to get our breath. He pointed high above the city to the remnants of a tower.

"Now, that *torre* or tower is round but whenever you see square towers, know they are from the Normans. There are many of them along the coast, as watch towers, on all of the lands they took over."

Aha, I thought. *I was just wondering about that.* I was stumbling along the cobblestones trying to keep up with Michel and to hear his every word, but he was a nonstop recording on the move. *Dash it all! What did he just say?*

When we finally arrived at the stairway to the Duomo, I took another deep breath. We had been climbing up the winding streets, and now we were to climb—yes, sixty-two steps—up to the church itself.

"The cathedral dates to the eleventh century," Michel said, as he began to tell us of the black and white exterior and the influence from the Moors, the Byzantines, and the Normans. Unfortunately, his voice was low, so I'm not certain what I picked up. Crowds of tourists swarmed around us, pushed by us, and languages from all countries converged and assailed us as we made our way inside the Duomo.

" . . . the interior is adorned in the late Baroque style with a nave and two aisles divided by twenty columns," I heard Michel say.

"The gold caisson ceiling has four large paintings that depict the flagellation of Saint Andrew, the miracle of Manna, the crucifixion of Saint Andrew and the Saint on the cross. Yes, after traveling and evangelizing all over what is now Turkey, and up into Russia, Andrew was eventually crucified in Greece in the city of Patras in the Peloponnese. Much later, his body, or his supposed remains, were brought to Constantinople, as Andrew had been made the patron saint of that great city, as well."

"Andrew really got around, didn't he?" Win whispered. I, too, was trying to understand what kind of travel took place back in the years following Christ's death.

"It's hard enough to travel now with all the modern conveniences," I whispered back. "I can't even imagine."

Michel then led us through the nave to point out a flight of stairs that led down to the crypt. "Below you will find the reliquary with Saint Andrew's remains. They were brought to Amalfi from Constantinople. During the fourth Crusade, the bloody and tragic sack of Constantinople in 1204 took place, in which the Eastern Orthodox Church was removed from the throne of Constantine's original seat of Christianity. It was during this time that one Cardinal Pietro Capuano, a fellow Amalfitan, fled for his safety, and in so doing, spirited Saint Andrew's relics back here to Amalfi. That is how St. Andrew's relics came to be used to stem the tide, so to speak, in 1343 against the seaquake."

"Aaahh," we all said, nodding, as if it all now clearly made sense. Michel led us through the Church, pointing out frescoes and other works of art that had come with various conquering forces and influences. Rounded-arched doorways signified Norman influence; pointed arched doorways signified the Moorish influence.

"You see these doorways? These arches? Similar design," Michel said, "can be found in the courts of palaces throughout the Middle East. Think Constantinople. Think Timbuktu."

Following Michel out of the softened, cool light inside the

cloister, we were immediately assaulted by the harsh September sunlight and the midday heat. I was grateful to be able to duck in and out of the darkened alleys in order to take advantage of any shade, or lingering morning chill, as we followed our fearless leader up a myriad of steps through the main part of town. The business section fell away as the steep canyon walls began to narrow and the roadway leveled out. We were following an ancient riverbed into a canyon.

Shortly, we arrived in the Valley of the Mills, a quiet, picturesque area with subtropical foliage, ferns, trees, and the remnants of ancient paper mills. I thought this was a perfect place to sink down for a picnic, but we were there for a different purpose.

"The Valley of the Mills," Michel said, "was once the center of a particularly important and flourishing business. The business of papermaking. Amalfi was one of the first in all of Europe to lead in making paper."

He stepped inside a doorway and waved us into a room that held dusty vats and bins, plus ancient water-driven wooden rollers, spindles, and wheels. He called out across the room. Bent over a large metallic sink, the figure of a man—possibly in his eighties and maybe five feet tall—turned his attention our way. A look of surprise shot in our direction. I stepped back. Few faces can launch a thousand ships, but this sweet but craggy face evoked images of characters found only in Dickens. A bulbous red nose projected from between piercingly blue eyes on his pallid, yet deeply lined face—a face encircled with bushy white hair. Hair sprang out in all directions, from his head, his enormous handlebar mustache, his eyebrows, his sideburns, and deep within his sizeable ears. Then, a twinkle lit his eyes, and I'm sure, if we could have seen his mouth, a smile formed. The sleeves of the man's rumpled blue plaid shirt, which were rolled above his elbows, revealed slender, yet slightly contorted arms that extended down into a tub of milky-white water. As he remained in place, his arms moved in a fluid motion, an activity honed by years, perhaps generations, of experience. Gently, he lifted a screen from the pulpy white water, shook it back and forth easily, tapped it, allowed the water to strain away, then moved with ease to a stack of dark brown cardboard, where he flipped the strainer, and produced—*Allora!*—a piece of handmade paper.

"You are witnessing the ancient art of papermaking," Michel announced, as he described the gentleman's movements. "This art came to us through the Arabic influences of centuries ago and was one of the crafts Amalfi refined and gave to the rest of Europe. The original Arabic paper, known as *bombacina,* supposedly came from the Arabian city of El Mambig, where they made paper from flax and hemp rags. The Amalfitans improved on this product and placed their own coat of arms on the paper as a guarantee of its high quality."

Michel passed around a thick, textured sheet of cream-colored, deckled-edged, handmade paper. Images of some of the finest stationer's shops in London and Paris loomed in my mind. I turned the paper over, ran my finger up and down the smooth sheet, turned it yet again, then passed it on to Winston. A letter or document written on such fine paper lent significance. Only a red wax seal with a ruling family's crest imprinted on the back was missing. Or, perhaps, the coat of arms of Amalfi would suffice. Quite impressive.

Following the demonstration, our tour group wandered back into the dappled autumnal light. A light breeze shimmered through the leaves slightly. The heat of the town and lower valley was now a mere memory. The air felt much more pleasant. Again, a picnic came to mind. I was hungry, but others at that moment had different thoughts. A voice from the back of the crowd asked, "Where are your townspeople buried?"

"Oh," he said, "you've asked a most pertinent question." Michel's dark eyes twinkled, and a mischievous smile passed over his swarthy face. He had us turn to face up the steep canyon, where we could make out winding paths that crisscrossed the almost vertical hillsides.

"This is a very serious thing we have to contend with," he said, contorting his eyebrows into dark furry ridges. "You see, because there are floods, seaquakes, and the like, we have concluded over the ages that we must bury our dead high up on the mountainside—way up there," he said, waving his small hand before our faces.

"So, when it comes time for the dearly departed to be transported up the mountain in a heavy casket, four or six of the strongest members of the deceased's family take hold of the handles, and after hefting and heaving the casket into a comfortable carrying position, they begin their long slow trek up to the burial site." He paused and turned around to face us.

"Timing is of the utmost importance," he said with great seriousness. "It is the job of the priest to waylay the family for, say ten minutes, twenty minutes, maybe more, depending on how heavy the casket is. Or, how heavy the deceased was. You see, it's not unusual for the pallbearers to take to swearing, and hollering, then laughing, and forgetting the reverential side of their job. And, of course, if the family were to proceed any too readily, they would be met with a round of cursing that would only undermine all that is or was holy. And I imagine the priest would have to do a flurry of new blessings to send the body to his or her proper place." Michel tilted his head to the side. A twinkle lit up his eyes, and his broad smile returned.

As we returned to town, Michel pointed out this shop, that curiosity, when he abruptly walked into a produce market that prominently featured lemons.

"Now, after all these centuries of international trade and crafts that support our livelihood, this lemon," he said, as he lifted one the size of a grapefruit, "has become one of our major sources of income—the *sfusato amalfitano,* or the lemons from Amalfi. Especially when made into our famous liqueur limoncello, which draws the international trade. Have any of you sampled this nectar of the gods?"

My husband and I nodded vigorously, but then slowed down our bobbing, just in case he was offering tastings to those who had *never* crossed into the world of appreciation of this succulent yet potent drink.

"First, let me have you taste the lemons themselves." As if a silent command had been emitted into the air, a plate of sliced lemon wedges arrived from the back room in the hands of an earnest and lovely young fruit seller. She moved gracefully through the throng, brushed a lock of dark wavy hair from her sweet face, and passed the plate around. The lemons were double the size of regular lemons, elongated in shape and with a thick, wrinkled skin. We each hesitatingly took a bite, expecting an immediate pucker. Ah, but the lemons were surprisingly sweet, very juicy, with few seeds. Then, as if serving us Holy Communion, a small thimbleful of liquid sunshine was dispensed by the lovely fruit seller to all of us willing and eager penitents. Like bobble heads, we nodded in approval, as the limoncello-filled bottles surrounding us begged for our attention.

Then Michel raised his hand and pointed up the steep valley to the hills that practically hung above Amalfi. He was preparing to tell just one more tale. We leaned in closer as he raised his voice.

"You've noticed the terraces high up on the mountains, haven't you?" We all indicated we had. "We have grown both olives and lemons for many centuries along those terraces. But, because there were few roads on the slopes, have you wondered how the produce was brought to the ships waiting in the harbor?"

As if auditioning to be participants on a TV show, we all looked at each other with perplexed expressions, then took up the head nodding again. Oh, he had us! We were putty in his hands!

"Years and years ago, before roads were built up and over the Amalfi peninsula, the only way people got from one place to another was by boat, or by hiking up and down the narrow vertical ascents and descents. It has always been a precarious matter getting from one place to another."

Again, Winston and I affirmed his comments, as our thoughts simultaneously flew to last night's madcap bus journey careening up the peninsula. I gulped. My husband stretched his neck and pulled his shirt collar away from his throat. The memory made it difficult to breathe as those heart-in-the-throat moments coursed through each of us. I realized we were still in survival mode.

"So, it was young ladies," Michel continued, "who were given the challenge to carry the lemons down to the awaiting ships. I would imagine the same took place for olives, but right now, I'll tell you about lemons. The fruit growers' sons were responsible for the harvesting of the lemons, but it was the young women who were sent racing down the mountain at full speed. Now, how did they do it?"

Again, the backroom curtains parted, and in returned the lovely fruit peddler, who was carrying a wicker basket of sorts. It was long, narrow, and cylindrical in form, with a wooden stave that was fastened with a leather strap to a circular band and extended about twelve inches up from the top of the basket. The fruit seller placed the band around the top of her head and swung the basket to her back and lashed the basket to her body with additional straps. Almost like Vanna White, she waltzed about the narrow fruit stall demonstrating the latest (or earliest in this case), in suitable workaday attire.

"You see," Michel said, drawing the young woman to his side, "in this way, the lemons were placed into this basket or into sacks —sometimes gunny sacks—and the women fastened the apparatus tight enough to be able to easily run down the steep slopes. Now you ask, why did they run?" He didn't wait for our answer.

"Once the ships were filled with the fruit, the young women were paid, and the ships could leave port. So, it was imperative for the gals to make certain that their produce made it to the boat in time. Plus, they were paid a bonus for their speedy delivery: their fathers could lift their heads high, along with their coin purses, because their fruit had been sold and was on its way to lands far away. Interesting, isn't it?" Again, we did the polite thing. We nodded. "Now, do I have any takers to carry the next load of lemons?"

We all laughed appreciatively as Michelangelo disbanded our tour. After thanking him, we all eagerly scurried through the shop to purchase the coveted bottles of limoncello we had been led there, like lemmings, to buy. The young fruit seller moved into her next act, by carefully wrapping each precious bottle in tissue, as her knowing smile, as well as her coffers, swelled. This was the end of their daily theatrical appearance.

After hauling our limoncello and the birthday barometer back to our hotel room, we quickly stripped down to something much cooler, packed our swimming suits, and headed down to the beach. A cooling dip in the Bay of Amalfi followed by a leisurely lunch at Stella Maris, an absolutely divine seafood restaurant, was just what the doctor ordered. A little *Risotto al Pescatore* and a glass of white wine—a lovely *Fiano di Avellino*— was superb. Oh, life was sweet!

CHAPTER THIRTEEN
A Trip to Pompeii

 he next morning was gray and drizzly, but after another hearty British breakfast of grilled tomatoes, bacon, and eggs at our British-owned hotel, we made our way down to the bottom of the city to—yes, that's right, to get back on the bus at the terminal. This time we were joining another tour group to travel from Amalfi over the top of the Sorrentine Peninsula and down the other side, where we would sidle along the Bay of Naples before a run up to Pompeii. Lorenzo was our tour guide, and he, too, was a colorful gent. Wiry, balding, with a fringe of yesteryear's dark hair, he introduced himself, hoisted his closed umbrella high over his head, and began to give instructions before we climbed onto the bus.

"Shortly, you are going to find yourselves in the amazing city of Pompeii, built, they believe, between the seventh and eighth centuries BC. The famous eruption of Mt. Vesuvius, which buried Pompeii, happened hundreds of years later during AD 79. Because Pompeii is so well-known and popular, you will find that the area is quite crowded. You will need to memorize not only the color of my umbrella," he said, lifting his red umbrella high, "but, you will also need to memorize my name, Lo-ren-zo, and the bus number, which is 54. Can you remember that much?"

Well, I believe we thought we could, and we all clambered aboard, as if all instructions were firmly in place. The weather continued to look a bit dreary; dark clouds—actually, fog—swirled up and about as we ascended over the pass in as harrowing a ride as our first drive up the coast. This time the driver was navigating narrow curves through mountains, with visibility sometimes diminishing to only a few meters ahead of us. Again, our ride was accompanied by the joyful honking of the horn each time we crept near a curve.

Winston slunk down into his seat and murmured, "They would have to come and tow the bus away if the horn broke down."

"At least we aren't dangling off cliffs over the sea," I said. But what were we dangling over? We had no idea, as we couldn't see. Too foggy! A memory flashed of a story a college friend of mine told me years before, while working as a tour bus driver in the Colorado Rockies. "Driving over Trail Ridge, at the Continental Divide, I would tell my passengers not to worry when they looked deep into the gorges below. 'There's nothing to see way down there, except old tour buses with bad brakes!'" I inwardly gasped. My memory was working overtime.

Our destination, Pompeii, conveniently sat at a railroad stop, or perhaps it worked the other way around. Whatever. If you came down for the day from Rome, you could simply catch a train, hop off in Pompeii, go on tour, and return to Rome the same afternoon. Like magic.

But we were already on tour, and had arrived by bus, and were immediately surrounded by a thousand other busses in the parking lot.

"What is the bus number?" I asked Winston, as we disappeared into the throng.

"Fifty-Four! Just like 'Car 54, Where Are You?' Remember that old TV series?"

I figured if I held onto him, he could remember anyway he wanted. I was busy trying to keep up with Lo-ren-zo and his short red umbrella, which kept disappearing then reappearing within the crowd. Being short ourselves, I could see this was going to be a challenge. I envisioned a day as a human pogo stick, leaping into the air to catch sight of Lo-ren-zo's umbrella. Oh, my! And me wearing inappropriate leaping shoes.

Pompeii was much larger than I expected, and we were herded like a gaggle of geese through enormous crowds, from one section of that amazing city to another. Imagine walking down the main thoroughfare, Via dell'Abbondanza. This wide stone boulevard, where ancient, but intact buildings lined the streets, and was named after the emerging classes who sought *abbondanza*, their own abundance in life. This road became the avenue where most of the city's commercial activities took place, where those who were not born into wealth made a living and eventually became wealthy as a result.

Looking more closely, I spotted traces of lava that seemed to have been swept aside for our benefit. (But how long ago?) The rectangular red brick buildings and houses (once whitewashed) all remained standing like forgotten soldiers at attention. From modest dwellings for simple workmen, or merchants who built their homes around their shops, to sumptuous villas, all had lined this street. Oddly, there were no windows in these buildings ready to greet us. The windows, it seemed, were built on the inside which opened onto an interior court or atrium.

"Depending on the wealth of the owner, lush gardens and mosaic-tiled reflective pools could have been there to greet you, instead of windows," Lorenzo explained. "But, let me start at the beginning," he said as he briskly pushed through the crowd and forged a way for our group to follow.

Lorenzo led us down to the Porto Marina. "I want to give

you the whole perspective, as this is where you, as a merchant or trader, would have entered Pompeii."

We faced a street which sloped steeply down a stone ramp that disappeared into a lush green field. No water. Just a green field. Curious, we all turned our attention back to Lorenzo.

"It was here that the Mare Tyrrhenum (our old friend, the Tyrrhenian Sea) swept through the Baio of Neapolis (Bay of Naples), up to the seawall and these outer gates of the city of Pompeii. As a trader, you would have made your way under sail to dock right here."

Again, we looked off to where the sea had once been but was at that moment at least five kilometers to the west. Cupping my hand over my eyes, I attempted to see back through time. *What would it have been like to sail up to this city in . . . what, 700 BC?*

As if reading my mind, Lorenzo said, "Like I told you before, Pompeii was established by the Oscans long before the Greeks founded nearby communities, such as Herculaneum, around the seventh to the eighth century BC. Once the Greeks made landfall, Pompeii eventually became absorbed into the Magna Graecia (Greek) way of life, as they learned to enjoy the culture, arts, and religion. As for the Romans, they simply took the art and architectural forms of their conquered peoples and made them their own."

"Didn't we read some of this history when we were in Florence? In Tuscany?" Winston asked me. I nodded. The history was beginning to come together.

In one brief statement, Lorenzo walked us through almost a thousand years of history. Our old friends the Etruscans, whom we had come to know the past week or so, along with the Greeks, had joined the Sabellines, on our tour south. (No, these are not the same as the Sabines we met in Florence.) I loved learning these details. So many influences flooding the shores at every turn.

Lorenzo continued, "This port entrance was established by the Romans. It was never the preferred entry by Pompeiians, but, as a merchant or trader, this is where you would enter with your goods to trade, animals to sell, or your animals to be used in the gladiator games. Turn around, and you will see the two Romanesque arches we just passed through. The larger one was specifically for large animals and the smaller one for pedestrians.

"Now, take a look at the stones under your feet. On our tour, you might spot some of these carved 'signs' along our route. What do you think they mean?" We each moved around in the crowd to peer more closely at the large flat stones he was pointing out. It appeared to be a strange shape carved into one stone.

"It isn't exactly an arrow, is it?" someone said.

Lorenzo grinned. We could tell he delighted in pointing out this "sign." "Actually, it is. This form, which was carefully incised into these stones, is in the shape of a phallus. It directed wayfaring sailors up from the old marina ramp and through the town to the neighborhood brothels." A twinkle flitted in his eyes as he turned to retrace our footsteps back inside the city wall. I glanced over at Win but kept my mouth shut. I could see we were in for a different type of tour than I expected. With raised eyebrows and a modicum of a puritanical lift to my step, I ambled along.

Traipsing back through the portals into the main part of the city and straight to the Forum, Lorenzo pointed out the layout of the facility. As my eyes swept up the few remaining Etruscan columns, my attention was briefly pulled beyond the city of Pompeii and into the nearby hills and Mt. Vesuvius. There, dark, foreboding clouds swirled about that ancient troublemaker. Surely a storm was brewing, and not far away. *Will we be forced to purchase yet one more umbrella?* The recent memory of buying an umbrella during a downpour in Florence flitted through my mind. And, also, in Milan. I started to make a joke with Winston, but he was intently staring at the stones along our path.

I, too, looked down at the well-worn stones (not looking for the phallus, mind you) but to take note of the smoothness and patterns of wear. For thousands of years, people had trodden upon this very place. I ran the toe of my shoe along the worn nooks and crannies of where I imagined wheels of oxcarts had been pulled. My eyes followed along a narrow trough where water had carved out permanent rivulets from centuries of rainy seasons.

Again, I looked up at the sky. Much of this wide expanse of the city held no cover; only a few buildings had roofs. No protection from the elements. Much had been destroyed by the flying cinders and lava flow of 79 AD. What had people thought or felt as the sky was literally falling in on them? I knew we would be seeing the life-form images in the Garden of the Fugitives, and I must admit the thought of seeing them was horrifying, yet I was oddly curious. In the meantime, what remained—or had been cleaned up—left little to the imagination. We moved along.

"The Temple of Apollo, which was built in the sixth century BC, was an integral part of the Forum, although the Temple predates the Forum." Lorenzo cleared his throat and waved his umbrella for our attention.

"The Temple holds architectural touches from both Greek and Italic (or Samnite) influences and you will see the remains of forty-eight Corinthian columns. The inner sanctuary, which is found up this long flight of steps," he said, with a sweep of his hand, "also has a myriad of columns along with a sacrificial altar opposite the main entry."

"Sacrificial altar?" I whispered to Win. Hopefully the sacrifices didn't include humans, as with the Etruscans.

"Because Apollo was the Greek god of gods, this building was at one time ornately decorated. But, like all décor and outward appearances, over time the color and/or ornamentation ceased to hold sway." Whew. No more mention of sacrifices.

From the Temple of Apollo, we ventured back through the Forum and up to the lovely Temple of Jupiter. "Originally built in the second century BC in honor of Jupiter, Juno, and Minerva, this temple became the main center for religious life."

From there we made our way into the Macellum, a type of market, and over to the old Modesto Bakery, where four large corn-grinding mills sat silently in front of a building. Brick ovens lay in wait for yet another round of bread to be baked. Those days had passed. As if our appetites hadn't already been whetted by journeying through the marketplace and bakery, we then entered the House of Ariadne. Not many tourists were in this house, so I began to relax. Up to that point, we had been herded from place to place, among thousands of tourists, who were all vying for the same spot to stand, take a photo, or catch a particular view. I thought we were handling the herding well, though I knew we both longed to be off on our own. We jealously watched small tour groups pass by us or those on self-guided audio tours, and Win said, "Next time. Next time, that's what we'll do."

Lorenzo had been talking as we walked, and I caught him in mid-sentence. "And this is one of the oldest houses in Pompeii and is also known as the House of Colored Capitals," he said. Before he showed us around, he zipped back out the door, clearly on a mission. We trampled along and turned the corner behind him—into the *lupanar,* the brothel. Oh, my!

With giggles and titters commingling with ogling, we realized we were now in the House of Pleasure. The crowds inside this two-story house were among the largest. Why, the pushing and gouging were the greatest discomfort we had experienced to that point. But we dutifully waited our turn to see the *piéce de résistance*: walls splashed with colorful murals of sexual attentions, including a "menu" of positions offered "for the pleasure of all men."

Lorenzo corralled us into a corner and continued speaking over the din of the pressing crowds. "The word *lupanar* or brothel comes from the word *lupa*, who were the women who called down from upstairs to lure the men to come up to them." We were not allowed to see any of the rooms upstairs but were told even though they were quite small and overly dismal, their walls were also covered in writing and scenes showing "amorous embraces." Amorous embraces would have been more acceptable then certain options displayed on the "menu plan," but then, who am I to complain? As my more modest thoughts eased, I realized the menu was probably an efficient plan. I could imagine a male customer saying, "I'll take two of those; one of those; and finish up with . . ."

We took a few photos and departed. Just as we stepped back into the street, I spotted one of the notorious stones. It had been there all along, lighting our way: the sign for "wayward sailors." I guess advertising had been helpful in years past—if there were no crowds blocking the signs.

Striding up the street once again, we pushed our way through the throngs to keep up with our group, taking on all the defensive measures we had encountered that morning. The crowds were getting larger and the pathways narrower. We found ourselves moving quickly toward the Stabian Thermal Baths. Now, Winston and I had seen a few of these the week before—in Fiesole, the Roman/Etruscan village above Florence. But most of those baths had been damaged, and it had been difficult to figure out the construction or the layout.

"Here you will see the oldest thermal baths in Pompeii," Lorenzo droned on. "A later version, called the Central Thermal Baths, can be found up the street and is considered their modern equivalent of the same thing. We may have time to see those later. But, for now, the Stabian Baths, named by the Samnites who began this construction, house a cold bath (*frigidarium*), a tepid bath (*tepidarium*), and a hot bath (*caldarium*). The Romans also added their own touches, which you will see, when they first conquered Pompeii. Take note of the beautiful plaster decoration along the walls."

Lorenzo's voice reverberated against the ancient walls, so we heard only every third word or so, but we continued to move en masse with him through the barrel-arched rooms, which had served the public's bathing needs. Stone benches lined the walls of every room. Windows high up near the ceiling let in light and probably rain in the steamy caldarium. Large stone pools and enormous sinks were still intact, which enabled us to appreciate how the water had flowed, and to understand the purpose of each space and activity that had taken place within the rooms. I sat down on one of the benches and let my mind wander. *What was it like to experience this opulent and yet important aspect of Roman (Stabian) life?* Before answers came, we were on the run again.

We followed Lorenzo into a large open room within the baths, where we were surprised to see a glass case which held one of the plaster "impressions." I wasn't prepared for this, but there he was. The cast was of a Pompeian man who had died in 79 AD during the Mt. Vesuvius' eruption. Must have been found right there in the baths, but he looked almost peaceful, as if he had just fallen asleep and failed to wake.

I must say that up to this point on our tour, we had seen little evidence of this horrific event. We were almost shielded

from the thoughts of it. Nevertheless, there are no words to describe how this stirs the heart. Yes, we knew we would be seeing
more impressions, but nothing had prepared me for how daunting an impact this would be. Suddenly, I felt heavy—heavier
than I had been five minutes before.

Stumbling out into the fresh air, the sky had finally light-
ened, and the gloom and clouds above Mt. Vesuvius had lifted—
at least for the time being. I felt relief. We continued again at a
fast clip, as if we had a bus to catch. Yet we seemed to be crisscrossing back and forth through this town; up one cobbled
street, down another, skirting Via dell' Abbondanza, but passing
places we'd just seen. There must have been a method to this
madness on Lorenzo's part, but I was beginning to wear thin. The
humidity level had risen as the wind dwindled. The sun was hot.

Lorenzo disappeared into another villa, (as most all these
houses are considered villas), so we could witness once again the
display of wealth the owners had accumulated throughout the
ages. "First is the House of the Faun," he stated, "which dates to
the fifth century BC. This was one of the most prestigious villas
in Pompeii and is said to have been owned by the nephew of
Sulla, a prominent general and statesman in Rome."

We walked around the atrium, which had a replica of a
bronze statue in the center of the reflecting pool. It was of a dancing faun. "The faun is known in mythology as a lustful Roman
god of the fields and woods, and is always half-man, half-goat
with a goat's horns, ears, legs, and tail. The original sculpture,
which is now housed in the Archeological Museum in Naples, is
one of the few remaining examples of ancient statuary."

We next visited the *House of Vetti*, where we were immediately greeted at the front door by a colorfully painted fresco
featuring a man with a penis the size of a modern-day baseball
bat. *This makes the brothel look tame*, I was thinking. Lorenzo

explained to us that this is Priapus, a "typical pornographic sign of fertility," and was purported to ward off evil influences. I'm thinking it might ward off puritans of all sorts, but other than that I can't compute how this "sign of fertility" would work in reverse psychology.

Villa Vetti was in beautiful condition and was certainly one of the best-preserved houses in Pompeii. The roof of this rectangular-shaped house, surrounding the atrium on four sides, had been completely rebuilt to show the true beauty of the home. It also protected the frescoes of the Cupids and Psyche, on the walls that surrounded the atrium and the charming statues scattered around the garden. The frescoes of mythological scenes throughout the house were still quite vivid in detail and color: depictions of pastoral scenes, Perseus and Andromeda, Ariadne and Dionysus, Daphne and Apollo; plus one entire room famous for the Cupid frieze: cupids making wine, working as goldsmiths, selling perfume from amphorae . . . were all simply charming. The delicate detail of the frescoes was most incredible—many painted directly on black backgrounds with crisp, clear gold-leaf flourishes and offset with bright red walls. I was enchanted.

By the time we left Villa Vetti, we were becoming weary and hungry. We needed a break. We breezed past the Thermopolium of the Phoenix, which once had served refreshing drinks to those at gladiator games. Oh, if it had only been open. Just to have a nice glass of . . . wine, perhaps? Water would do, too. We trudged on. We were near the amphitheater, but didn't go in. Time was short.

Instead, we found ourselves in the Garden of the Fugitives, where thirteen impressions were lined up on the ground in the positions they had been when the lava had brought them down. As if still in flight as they had tried to outrun a fiery death from the molten lava, the plaster impressions showed their very last movements before being overtaken. With pain still visible on their faces, we found families clustered together with mothers clutching children to their breasts. All were trapped with no way to escape. Again, we were bereft. It was then that I realized why this experience had been left to the last of our tour. The impact had knocked the breath from me.

As Lorenzo began to explain the scene, I tried to imagine the experience. I glanced out the door to Mt. Vesuvius. "At first, there were towers of debris drifting to earth in fine-grained ash," Lorenzo said, "then lightweight chunks of pumice and rock. It must have been terrifying. Pliny wrote of that time, 'I believed I was perishing with the world, and the world with me.' But the fact that he could recount this scene meant he had, indeed, escaped. Pompeii was where the most devastation from this historic event took place. It has been written that 'a pyroclastic surge'—a 100-miles-per-hour upwelling of superheated poison gas and pulverized rock—poured down the side of the mountain and swallowed everything and everyone in its path. All succumbed within minutes."

As we walked back to the exit and prepared to leave Pompeii—quite an amazing place of antiquity—I looked back over the city. Much of the time during our tour, I had kept my eyes down, so I would not stumble or miss an "errant sailor" sign. But I suddenly was aware of all the places we hadn't visited. I was exhausted, yet there was still so much more to see. Next time. As good as dear Lo-ren-zo was as a guide, next time, my husband told me, we'll come tour on our own. We collapsed back into the bus and headed to some place up the road for lunch. The food was typical of most tour lunches: maudlin fare in a clamorous environment slap dashed onto your plate along with a splash of local vino into your waiting glass. We ate very little.

As our tour bus prepared to drive to the top of Mt. Vesuvius, the clouds began to rumble and the rain that had threatened us all morning finally arrived with great force. Cold rain made rivulets down the dusty bus windows, and the moment we arrived at the top, we could see—nothing! It felt like clouds were hanging on top of our shoulders. We could not make out anything more than ten feet from the bus, so we were saved from having to face that fiery dragon that wiped out the lovely city we had just visited. I was relieved. I could not handle any more of Mt. Vesuvius's wrath. Despite having to return to the Amalfi Peninsula on the steep and incredibly winding road, I looked forward to getting back.

Once we arrived back in Amalfi late that afternoon, the sun popped out as if welcoming us home. We automatically wandered down toward the sea, which was just a stone's throw away. And, yes, there was our favorite lovely trattoria perched above the beach—Stella Maris—calling seductively. We climbed the steps and were immediately settled onto the deck, where we ordered a couple of glasses of the same local white wine we had discovered the day before. We needed to loosen up and shake off the day's travails. We looked around us. The atmosphere was as congenial as the day before, the wait staff was friendly, and oh my . . as waiters breezed past, followed by the intoxicating aroma of a garlic-infused broth of *cozze* (mussels), we couldn't resist ordering. The thought of facing an evening meal of bland Brit food back at the hotel was out of the question. But our appetites had returned.

We shared a large bowl of cozze as an appetizer, then ordered the fresh *pasta alla vongole* (with clams). Scrumptious! It was a night to revel in, one in which to relax. It was a perfect evening to sip wine in a most embracing part of the world. Visions of Pompeii drifted away on the adjoining surf.

CHAPTER FOURTEEN

Isola di Capri, The Island of Love

*T*he following morning, Amalfi was awash with sunshine. We bounded down the steps from the hotel and into the center of Amalfi before continuing farther down toward the busses. But this time we bypassed the bus terminal and stood eagerly awaiting our next trip—a boat tour to the island of Capri.

Boats of all shapes and sizes roared in and out of Amalfi— some old fishing trawlers that dawdled noisily up to the shore; some hydrofoils, looking like water spiders as they danced in and out of the waves; and then, our stalwart tour boat with room for ten thousand of your closest friends. We clambered aboard and made our way to the top deck where we found seats in the open air. Like wiggly puppies, we fidgeted about, as we were both excited to be out on the water and embarking on this new adventure. The sun streamed across the water, setting the waves afire. The sky was crystalline. No morning fog, no marine layer caressing the shore, nothing but pure clarity to witness all the world had to offer.

Our boat skirted west along the southern coast of the Amalfi Peninsula at a fast clip, the wake churning behind us in reckless abandon. We gaped at the steep cliffs along the coastline and were oh so glad we were not continuing our trip by bus. We breathed in a sigh of relief. High above us on those precipices, ancient villages clung to the rocks like lichen. Ten miles farther, the engines throttled down, and we slowed to turn toward the mainland, then inched slowly up to the beaches of Positano. We had arrived to pick up more passengers.

Rising above the coastline and virtually cleaving to vertical rock formations, Positano is said to be the quintessential picturesque seaside village. One cannot help but be astounded at the beauty, yet marvel at the skill and tenacity of those who chose to build on such crags. Positano is also known to be one of foremost exclusive seaside resorts in Italy. The beaches beyond the port were sprinkled with colorful beach chairs and umbrellas along with inviting trattorias.

Win turned toward me and spoke over the sound of the engines. "Given the opportunity, we could find out if this little gem lives up to her reputation." I nodded assent. I would love to visit Positano.

Once new passengers had boarded, the engines began winding up again and the thrust of the boat tossed us backward. We laughed with surprise. More folks were trying to find seats on the top deck. We decided to venture down below, as creatures always do on boats (up, down, in, out, people are always on the move on a boat). I decided to hang out on the stern. Hovering over the port side and closer to the water, the cooling spray made me feel giddy and exuberant. The wake churned white and billowed behind us, as if we had plowed through a bank of snow. We left the protection of the peninsula and headed to the southwest and back into the Tyrrhenian Sea. (Yes, I should have named this book, *Tales along the Tyrrhenian Sea*.) The color of the water was so blue, I took off my sunglasses to see if my eyes were playing tricks. No, the color was azure and the water so clear, I swore if we had slowed down, we could have made out the bottom.

Winston called my name and I made my way over to join him on the starboard side of the stern. We were getting closer to a massive rock that seemed to be rising out of the sea. Yes, it was glorious Capri, looming like not one island but two joined at the hip in friendship. Just then, a jaunty yellow submarine popped up not far from us, and we realized we were in for a circus of experiences.

Win grinned. "Here we are! Two lovers of Italy and two lovers of boats and water out to see Capri!" he bellowed over the roar of the engines.

Our boat pulled into a broad, curving bay on the north side of the island. We had entered a deep-water harbor known as Marina Grande and were, surprisingly, not alone. No joke. There must have been a hundred tour boats arriving besides ours and at least a thousand people disgorging from each boat. I heard Winston gasp, like he was hyperventilating. This was our third day of organized tours, and he had already determined that the word "tour" was a four letter word. Our guide, O-What's-his-name, spoke in so many different languages and at such a fast pace, we failed to catch his name or some of his directives. I tried to sidle closer. He carried a bright blue umbrella, which he thrust up and down into the air like a piston and called out in a high-pitched voice, "Ca-pri tour! KA-pri tur!" Had he not considered that all of us were on a Ca-pri tour? Even years later, those words conjure up memories of the "cattle call" we responded to that day.

The glorious morning was already turning hot. Steam was rising off the pavement along the docks. While we awaited more specific directions for taking yet another tour bus, we began to shed our sweaters and jackets and repacked the backpack. (Yes, there were three umbrellas in there.) Hawkers were pitching tickets to take a boat tour around the island, some to see the

Blue Grotto sea cave; others for private convertible taxis. The din from the noise rose with the heat.

"Capri is known as the Pearl of the Tyrrhenian Sea," Reynaldo said. (I had gotten closer to read his name tag.) "Or, the Island of the Sirens, as the Sirens, those mythological sea nymphs, were said to have lived here. And since Sirens have crowded men's fantasies for all eternity, then this, you'll see, is the island of their most capricious dreams," he said with a wild sweep of his umbrella.

We relaxed into Reynaldo's latent charms and looked around. Slightly to the east of the marina, was a funicular, or tram. My eyes followed the upward sweep of the cars on the funicular as they traveled straight up the steep mountain to the crest of the peak high above us. There, I assumed, was where we would find the village of Capri. Our view from the bottom was spectacular. I couldn't imagine the sight we would behold from the top.

Our tour group divided up and scrambled onto small shuttle busses. No funicular for us, I guess. We overheard mumbles, grunts, and grumbles as couples were herded in one way, then another. The shuttles took us up the coastal road, the Via Marina Grande. We drove past the turn to *Palazzo a Mare*, (the ancient Roman villa of Emperor Augustus), the entrance to the *Grotto Azzuro* (Blue Grotto), and past the signs for the *Bagni di Tiberio*, (the Baths of Tiberius). Why, we wondered, were we missing out on all those treasures? The road was snake-like, with ten—count them, ten—hairpin turns as we climbed up the steep mountainside. Thick foliage along the route made it difficult to see the hidden villas we were told were lurking behind the next stand of cypress, umbrella pines, mastic, or myrtle trees. Instead of leveling off and going on to Capri, we made a 180 degree turn and continued toward the village of Anacapri.

Sadly, we also eased past the supposed Barbarossa Castle,

where we might have seen rounded towers and broken walls that remained. Reynaldo boomed out over the PA system, "The castle, dating from the tenth century, fell into disrepair when the Turk Barbarossa invaded this island in 1535. He ended up destroying the very castle named after him." (Or maybe it was the other way around, and the castle was named after its destruction. Something was lost in translation, as we were hearing only the English.)

"Is there another way to get up to Anacapri?" a fellow tourist, who was sounding a tad shuttle-sick, shouted to our guide.

"Yes, there is the Scala Fenicia, known as the 'Phoenician Stairway.' From Marina Grande, it is only eight hundred steps straight up." We all groaned and snugged down into our comfy shuttle seats. But as it turned out, we had just arrived at the pinnacle near Monte Solaro and the village of Anacapri. We popped off the shuttle in the Piazza Vittoria (Victory Plaza).

"This is the second largest town on the island, and even though it is 570 feet above the sea, it has been a town since prehistoric times. Although the only way up here before 1877, was . . . yes, the Scala Fenicia. For several thousand years, all commodities were carried up by the women of Capri on top of their heads. Their beauty was purported to be an object of great admiration," Reynaldo said, tears glistening in his eyes.

I shook my head. (How was it that if women were doing all the work, men had time to ogle? Allora!) As we made our way down a small path in search of a restroom, we also looked for an opening through the shops, the boutiques, and the thick foliage to catch a peek at the panorama. From some of the open spaces near the top, the views were breathtaking, as we could see far out to sea to the west and down below us to the east where Marina Grande appeared to be miniaturized. We were given time to walk through the village and then were taken down a garden path, literally. Surprisingly, the only thing I remember, other than the colorful foliage and flowers closest to the path, was the back of the blue plaid shirt on the tall man in front of us. He, too, was sweating. The heat had followed us, and even at this elevation we were taking off our caps, wiping our brows, and hoping for some shade, a spot of lunch, water, or all the above. Finally, we managed to get far out on a ledge of the garden hanging well above Marina Grande and were able to take some great photos. Mr. Blue Plaid Shirt had wheeled off into the shade of a row of cypress trees.

"Ca-pri tour! Ca-pri tour!" we heard our group leader call out. *È ora di pranzo!* Time for lunch! Like the herd of cattle we all had become, we clopped after Reynaldo in search of lunch and a place to sit down out of the heat. We were greeted at our designated restaurant by an elderly gentleman, Bacchus, wearing a Roman toga with a sprig of grape leaves in his hair and grapes drooping over his shoulders.

"*Bené!* Then, there must be *vino*," Winston whispered to me in his best Italian. We followed Bacchus inside. The restaurant was used to serving large tour groups, and tables stretched from one room to the next. The food began to appear as soon as we were seated. Other than a lovely, fresh *Caprese salad* (fresh buffalo mozzarella, freshly sliced tomatoes, fresh basil leaves, all sprinkled liberally with local olive oil, a splash of balsamic vinegar, and salt and pepper), the rest of the food, which was a pasta course and some steamed vegetables, seemed overly heavy in the heat and, unfortunately, not memorable. But, taking Bacchus's lead, we did have a small carafe of cool rosé, which took the sting out of the heat from the day.

Shortly after our *pranzo*, we were herded back into the shuttles and taken a few short miles to the main village of Capri. The town lies in the saddle of land between Monte Solaro to the west and Monte Tiberio (Tiberius) to the east. Far below us was our old friend, Marina Grande, and off the steep backside of the island was Marina Piccolo, with surf lapping at its toes.

Once we were let off the shuttle, Reynaldo told us to meet him in a couple of hours near the Piazza Umberto Primo. "See you back here under the Torre dell' Orologio."

The lovely clock tower he was referring to reigned over the main square near where we were dropped off. We looked longingly at the panoply of bistro tables that stretched elbow to elbow through the small square. I longed to sit and people watch with another cool glass of something, but this was our first trip to Capri. We had a lot to see and this might be our only chance to be on our own.

"Is this not the island of love?" Winston asked me with a bit of a swagger. I flashed him my best cheeky smile, and we began to wander off. As we crossed the piazza, the gleaming white baroque façade of the Church of Santo Stefano greeted us. Large crowds were filing in and out of her doors, but we continued past. Ancient Roman aristocracy was calling us to check out their summer palaces, and we were eager students.

Built in a maze-like fashion, the streets and alleys crisscrossed one another by scooting up flights of stairs, zipping through arches, or spilling into smaller piazzas. Bougainvillea in hot fuchsia pinks and deep purples cascaded down the outside of white-washed buildings onto elaborate stone curlicues that graced low-hanging doorways, and along white stucco walls, often playing hide-and-seek with a myriad of roses of every hue. We were charmed, but there was also another . . . shall I say presence?

Earlier in the day, we had noticed the chic stores in Anacapri, but they barely held a candle to those in Capri. With every step we took, we were aware of the extreme wealth, and the ultra-elite who were being catered to in this very famous international village. Every boutique beckoned to clientele who had more than a few million in disposable lira (Euro) to their names. Brand names called out enticingly like barkers at a county fair: Louis Vuitton, Dolcé Gabbana, Prada, or Versace. Others less flamboyant in nature championed the ideal of "handmade from Capri," such as the exquisite jewelry from Tuccia, the bejeweled hand-crafted sandals of *Amedeo Canfora*, or the perfume-maker, who gathered local herbs and flowers to create his own fragrances at Carthusia. Need a Hublot or Vacheron Constantin watch? It could be found. Need a Maserati? That, too, could easily be acquired. But, if you were in the market for a simple souvenir or trinket to remember Capri, you best save your money until you reach the bottom of the mountain. There was nothing worth lugging around in that heat. Only a few shops with less than tasteful choices were tucked in along the way to balance out the wonder.

Restaurants, too, catered to an exclusive clientele. Hotel doors were discretely opened for the famous. Male movie stars—from countries of which we had no clue—sauntered down the streets and were obvious only by the bevy of beauties fawning all over them as paparazzi snapped pictures. Starlets, too, were equally encumbered by the ogling masses.

We turned down a side street and made our way out of the —nope, not madding, but maddening—crowd and followed Via Matteiotti to where one of the most famous of all residents of Capri had supposedly made his home and gardens: Augustus Caesar at the Gardini di Augusto. It seems that after the Greeks had spent centuries living here, Caesar Augustus was the first to discover the charm of Capri when he visited the island in 29 BC. It is said that he was so taken by the island's beauty that he traded the nearby fertile island of Ischia to the city of Naples. This marked the beginning of Augustan rule. His successor, Tiberius, embarked on an intense building program on Capri between the years of 27 and 37 AD, resulting in the construction of twelve villas.

The tranquil garden was a respite and was filled with luxuriant varieties of botanical plants and trees. Simply by stepping under the lush green canopy of umbrella pine, palm, cypress, and myrtle trees, the temperature lowered at least ten degrees. The paved garden paths wove in and around smaller islands of flowers—birds of paradise, carnations, petunias, pansies, geraniums—all interspersed with Greek statuary (maybe Roman). A centerpiece lily pond featured a modern bronze sculpture. Stone walls marched up the side of the hills where arched bridges cavorted—was that where Augustus lived? As it turned out, this all had been put in place in the early twentieth century by a German named Krupp! Sad, but true.

But the point that captures all imagination and beckons to be photographed from the gardens again and again is the view of Marina Piccolo to the south side of the island and the cobalt blue sea far below. Off to the east, majestic brown sea stacks known as the Faraglioni Rocks rise out of the water at least 100 meters (300 feet). Carved by wind, sea, and time, these rocks are so well-loved they have been named Stella (Star), Faraglione di Mezzo (in between), and Scopolo. Also, far below us and to the west of Marina Piccolo was another rock formation, known as Scoglio delle Sirene, or the Rock of the Sirens. It was once considered to be home to the sea nymphs of classical mythology. All along the south side of the gardens, rock ledges had been shaped for all to come, sit, dream, and fall in love with each other—and oh, with this little piece of heaven. Truly divine!

Peering below us, we spotted a serpentine-like path, known as Via Krupp, which had been cut out of the side of the mountain leading down to Marina Piccolo. I sighed. I could only sit and watch others brave their way down the long, winding road. Bad knees. Bad back. Supposedly, if we had gone, we could have seen an ancient Saracen tower while en route. I kept wondering what would happen if I had gone and couldn't make it back up. I saw no other roads, no cars, so I guess a boat ride around to the other side might have been in order to catch our tour boat. Or were there donkeys?

Speaking of boat rides, one thing on our Capri to do list, was to take a boat ride into the famous Blue Grotto, those stupendous caves off Marina Grande and the supposed personal swimming hole of Emperor Tiberius. Unfortunately, all the tour guides cautioned us—oh, how they cautioned us—because, if the surf was too turbulent, no boats would be allowed in the caves. Even if you were holding a ticket to venture into those spellbinding sapphire blue reflective caverns, you might be left holding the very ticket you had purchased and were never allowed to use. Being sailors, we were aware of how the afternoon winds could pick up and churn the waters. We didn't fall for the ruse.

We slowly meandered back up to the main piazza, the Piazza Umberto I, where we finally found a table to sit and sip—yes, sip—another glass of refreshing rosé under the lovely clock tower. Around us, *tutto il mondo* (all the world) continued to pass by.

"We'll simply have to return," I breathed. "Too much to see, too much to do, and next time . . . "

"Next time," Win picked up, "we'll travel on our own tour, at our own pace, and on our own timeline." Yes, he was so right.

Suddenly, we heard Reynaldo's voice "Ca-pri tour! Ca-pri tour!" calling from across the piazza. We gulped down the rest of our wine, paid, and again, like part of the herd we had become, headed back to the shuttle. There were some cattle calls we knew we must heed.

Once we returned to Amalfi, we trekked back over to our now favorite seafood restaurant ever, Stella Maris. Again, we were led to a table overlooking the sea—the sea on which we had just returned. And again, we settled into an evening of utter bliss with traditional food and our new favorite wine, Fiano di Avellino. This was our last night in Amalfi and we had learned to do things right!

To commemorate our enjoyment of these few days in Amalfi, we made our way across the street into a beautiful shop filled with hand-painted ceramics. A rainbow of delightful, brightly colored plates was splashed across the walls—all telling the story of Amalfi and Amalfitans: farmers picking lemons, fishermen pulling in nets, and vintners harvesting grapes. I was in heaven. The difficulty was in trying to choose, and then lugging the plates home. Fortunately, the friendly shopkeeper came to my rescue. She recommended the convenience of shipping. (What a novel idea!) Not certain my husband was in on this conversation, I realized I could choose . . . well, several.

Later, as we made our way back up the steps to the Amalfi Hotel, it dawned on us the US dollar amount we had just paid. "It's only lira!" I heard myself mumble. I had avoided learning how to do conversions.

CHAPTER FIFTEEN
On to Apulia

We boarded a bus from Amalfi back down to Salerno the following morning at six-thirty. Our time on the Amalfi coast and in the region of Campania was at an end. This day would be a triad adventure of sorts: first by bus, then by train, followed by car. Our destination was Porto Cesareo in Apulia. So, where is Porto Cesareo, you might ask? Good question. I wasn't clear on that concept either, except that was where we were scheduled to spend a full week at a timeshare. We figured it was located somewhere in the "heel of the boot" of Italy.

Once we arrived at the train station in Salerno, we were to catch a train to Brindisi via Taranto—going from the western most part of Italy to the Adriatic Sea on the east coast. Before our trip, Winston had carefully researched the best train schedules on the internet but had realized the night before that the tickets we had received were not the most direct route. (No, we did not want to go back up north to Rome to cut way back south to our destination.) Without understanding much Italian, Win wiped his hand across his brow and stepped up to the agent at the ticket booth. I stepped back out of the way while he placed the printouts from his internet finds upon the counter. The agent shoved his eight-inch-thick binder of train schedules aside

—no internet usage here—raised his two-inch-thick black eyebrows, and began to peruse the schedules my impertinent American husband had thrust before him. In due time, he opened the large binder, matched the schedules back and forth, and then shoved his hat back off his forehead and scratched his temple. A slight smile, not a full one, formed on his lips. He would not—could not—fully acknowledge the merit of my husband's finds, for he *was* Italian! (We were not there to make his life difficult; just to get better tickets.)

Just then, I felt a sharp jab on my back and was pitched forward toward the ticket line. I turned around and there in front of me was an elf of a woman—only four foot six at best—glowering up at me while screeching in a most unintelligible Italian. (Who am I kidding? To me, all Italian was unintelligible.) Her toothless mouth twisted into a grimace as she planted her hands on her slim hips and held her stance. The caked dirt on her creased face, hair, hands, and clothes told a story of neglect and homelessness. I stepped back embarrassed, but obviously not far enough. Again, she railed at me. And just in case I hadn't fully comprehended her message, this wizened little woman raised her mottled gray dress up over her head and waggled her scrawny and quite naked body at me. Ah, I now got the message! I had been standing with our luggage on a piece of cardboard in the corner of the railway station. Apparently, I had entered her home territory by mistake and was standing in her "living room." Embarrassed at having put this poor woman in a tizzy, I hurriedly grabbed our bags and inched closer to my husband in line.

"*Si, bene!*" I heard the ticket agent exclaim as he threw his hands in the air in a gesture of triumph. I was not certain what had been said before that, but I was sure it must have been, "Why, yes, there *is* a way to get from here to there!" And, in an expression of complete magnanimity, he exclaimed in English,

"And, your trip will not take you the prescribed twelve hours, but only seven!" He had found a way! Win turned to me with a grin of complete surprise and delight. Unaware of the trouble I had just caused, he scooped up our tickets and transfers for the day's journey. He was downright ecstatic at having completed this difficult transaction.

I glanced over my shoulder to where the old woman was still holding vigil and gulped. Just as I reached for my purse to offer penance, Win grabbed our bags from my hands and made for the door.

"We're running late," he said. I nodded at her, then stumbled after him, helping to drag our bags down two sets of stairs and back up two more sets in order to reach another platform where we would wait for our train—the train we were fearful of missing. My knees were still shaking from the odd happenstance with the woman. I felt mortified that I hadn't noticed the old woman before, but then she hadn't been in her "place of residence" when we arrived. The memory of her still breaks my heart.

For all the connections we made that day, and for all the hours we rode the train, we were fortunate to have food service—very limited, yet available. But, in late afternoon, we clambered aboard what turned out to be a most unusual train. Once we got moving, Win said excitedly, "Do you hear that?" I cocked my head to the side. The engine noise was deafening, so I couldn't hear anything else.

"Do you hear that?" he asked again. I had no idea what he was talking about, but his excitement was palpable.

"The engineer is shifting gears!" he said, wide-eyed. "Like in an old truck." His realization and disbelief almost sent him jumping from his seat.

Sure enough, as we chugged along to Taranto, "the little engine that could" shifted gears, as if in a standard-shift car. This little coal-driven train struggled to carry us along that precarious stretch of our journey. Some regular commuters sitting near us smirked; others smiled. Some attempted to tell us in limited English what was happening, but nothing translated. Each time we stopped at yet one more village, an unholy belch of black smoke jettisoned from the engine. The regulars simply shrugged, and smiled, as if to say, "This is our normal."

The train windows, which had been thrown open due to the heat of the day, sucked in the toxic coal smoke from the engine. Tourists like us were now visibly nervous and leaned their heads out the windows. The conductor, who had been diligently collecting tickets, also began frantically poking his head out the open window near us. Then, he raced down the aisle and out onto the tracks! Alarm was visible on many faces around us, as others—obvious commuters used to this line—rolled their eyes, threw their heads back, and laughed. We felt like unwitting actors in a silent movie with either Buster Keaton or the Keystone Cops. We couldn't decide whether to laugh, cry, or save ourselves by jumping off the train. A young woman reached over, patted my knee, and smiled. She kindly let us know this was all in a day's journey, and not to worry. *Non fartene un pensiero!* It happens all the time. We had no choice and settled back to enjoy this charade of a train trip.

Eventually, the train reached its destination, Brindisi, and with a deep inhalation of breath all of us tourists dragged our earthly belongings—or whatever we were traveling with—and made our way off the beleaguered train. We departed sadly though, as we had made a connection with some of the passengers. For a few moments we had felt no longer alone on this adventure in Southern Italy.

Brindisi, which lies on the Adriatic Sea along the eastern coast of Italy, is the far end of the Roman Appian Way, and is one point of departure for those sailing off to Greece. Many of the train's passengers were making their way to the port for their nighttime sail. I imagined—just across that narrow stretch of water was yet another land—the island of Corfu. Greece. Albania. Ah, but for another time.

Instead, we made our way to the car rental office and picked up a car. Then, we drove across the heel of the boot to the Ionian Sea, which was only about 58 kilometers, or 36 miles. We arrived at the hotel, Torre Inserraglio, our timeshare for the week, just as the golden light of day was setting in the west. After checking out our condo, we realized if we stood on one of the balconies, and if we stood on tiptoe, we could make out the small village of Porto Caesareo and the Ionian Sea beyond. It was already eight o'clock, so our concierge suggested we venture out to grab some pizza at one of the few open restaurants. We didn't stay late. It had been a very long day, so we sleepily headed back to the condo. The next day we would make our real discoveries.

And, indeed, we did. We awakened to a bright, sparkling day. Our apartment was quite modern, with a balcony off a large bedroom, a small bathroom with a shower, plus a kitchen, living room, and a second balcony. All the conveniences of home. But, once again, to make morning coffee, we had to learn the ways of yet one more kitchen stove and an impressive, unique Italian coffee pot. Patience is a virtue! That adage must have originated near here, or somewhere in the Mediterranean. Of that, I was certain. We flip-flopped our way out the door and down to ask the concierge how to make coffee—in English, *per favore*—and how to turn on the clever, yet interesting electric stove. The centigrade numbers and the oven dial with a 1, 2, 3 meant something to someone. Again, we were novices.

Next, we ventured into Porto Cesareo. The very name conjures up visions of Caesar, so we were determined to check out more than its grocery store. What we found was a small, barren fishing village. Yes, as described in the brochures we had read beforehand, there were narrow alleys (streets), whitewashed houses, bougainvillea, flowering vines, and a lively harbor. Were there seafood restaurants? No. It was Sunday, and to top that off, the tourist season had ended a few weeks before our arrival. We found a ghost town left in its place. We did discover the nearby town of Torre Cesarea. It was named after a large square stone coastal tower which hovered at the water's edge next to the beaches. It had been there for over a thousand years. But the beaches were closed for the season, even though some looked quite inviting. Smooth sand, crystal-clear waters, shallow depths . . . oh, well.

Our main goals were to find a post office and a grocery store. Again, we were faced with a new system of figuring out the local hours of service for both. This time, we had no Margarita from Poderi to help us decipher the special codes for Porto Cesareo's system. Unfortunately, the post office was not only closed but locked, padlocked, and chained for further effect. But it was Sunday. Fortunately, we found a grocery store just before it closed for the day at 1 p.m..

Sweat rolls off me even now as I remember with embarrassment that first day of grocery shopping in Caesareo. We were planning to be in the condo for a week, so we needed to purchase plenty of food and supplies. Sadly, I didn't remember what I'd learned while shopping with Margarita in Manciano: Don't handle the produce! Don't weigh your own tomatoes! Most Italian markets have people who will handle these matters for you; you are not to paw through their vegetables, pinch their peaches, or thump their melons. Nope! It's not to be done! Never!

As you can imagine, I was yelled at, as if I were a ten-year-old about to hightail it out of the store without paying. *Non toc-care questa roba!* Don't touch this stuff! *Non toccare questa roba!* Oh, Lordy! With tears leaking down my reddened face, I made my way to the dried pasta aisle, crouched down near the floor, and bawled, albeit quietly. How humiliating! *Is this the way they treat all tourists? Is the tourist season truly over?* Yes, it was, and the folks in that grocery store had run out of patience. Patience, it appears, is not a virtue once the tourist season is over. (If you've ever worked in a summer resort, you would understand. I have and I understood!)

Blotting my blotchy face dry with my sleeve, I stood up. It was then I realized the pasta aisle went the entire length of the store—with packages of pasta lining the shelves on both sides, in the most amazing shapes and sizes and with the most delightful names. None of these were like what I'd stumbled upon in Manciano; none of these had I seen before. I brightened. My mind went wild with the prospect of *orecchiette* (little ears pasta) prepared with wild sorrel and broccoli rabe; *cavatelli* (rolled flat coin-shaped pasta) served with bean soup and mussels; *macheroni* (a larger version of cavatelli) swimming in fresh tomato and meat ragú, and *sagne incannulate* (long, one-inch wide flat strands of pasta twisted as tight as curling-iron curls) served with lentils, tomato sauce, and a side dish of bitter greens glistening in local olive oil. Our shopping cart seemed to shrink in size as I piled in a week's worth of pasta-bilities.

That afternoon, we made our way down to Mare Ionio—the Ionian Sea—where we spent the afternoon relaxing and reading on a deck laid over an extremely rocky beach. The waves were crashing wildly, which prevented us from edging down the aluminum ladder into the waters. The beaches, large spans of dark gray volcanic rock, were impossible to walk directly upon, thus the importance and protection of the deck and stairs. Imagine molten lava boiling up into a frothy mass and solidifying into thorny spikes. Yikes! Wild, yet wonderful! But, making it difficult to move freely about.

That evening I tried my hand at preparing a dinner of *sagne incannulate* pasta with fresh tomatoes, bitter greens splashed with plenty of olive oil—and, of course, local red wine. A *Gioia del Colle* from Lecce, I believe. Win tuned in the radio and we were treated to a mix of Arabic music with an Italian accent. It was quite beautiful, yet exotic. Why not? We were closer to Albania than we had ever been, and not that far from the northern part of the African continent. Belly dance, anyone?

The following day was Win's birthday, and to celebrate we headed off in our car to discover what felt like a third world country. One step off the luxurious timeshare/hotel property and we were brought face to face with what appeared to be a millennium of poverty-stricken villages. The landscape was hardscrabble, with plenty of craggy rocks, and nothing but barren ground. Few farms sprouted up around us.

Once we turned off the narrow donkey paths called roads, we were suddenly swept up into four lanes of traffic heading pell-mell into a city called Lecce. Alarmingly, six lanes of traffic converged into four. Win grew extremely nervous as cars squeezed us in and out of lanes and it was difficult to tell what move he should make. Panic was beginning to set in—fast.

Somewhere hidden in my own fright, I asked him, "Where do you think the people in Boston came from?" Winston, who was born and bred in Massachusetts, grew up with, among others, the Irish, the Portuguese, and, of course, the Italians.

A light must have dawned because immediately he began to drive like he was heading away from Boston's Logan Airport just before being squeezed into Sumner Tunnel. He knew exactly how to drive and had no problem after that, waving his hand, gesturing, never looking anyone in the eye, and carrying it off with panache. Could I have driven there? Absolutely not. I grew up in Nebraska.

Lecce is an ancient city founded during prehistoric times by the Messapii, a Greek or Cretan group ruled by King Malennius. According to legend, the city of Lecce, once named Sybar, existed at the time of the Trojan War. Only much later in time did the Romans settle in this city, near the eastern-most point of the Via Appia which ends just north of Lecce in Brindisi on the Adriatic.

We parked the car and made our way on foot through the Porta Rudiae, (the gateway to the city), which commemorates saints along with the ancient pagan king, Malennius. On that day, we were in search of Roman ruins. We found two amphitheaters, but, because we had no local guidebooks for Lecce, we had no idea what else to look for. As we continued to walk, we saw art and architecture that revealed influences from the many invading forces which had passed through, including Byzantines and the Normans. We also discovered an astounding and amazingly beautiful inner city built with Baroque architecture (from the mid-thirteenth to the seventeenth century), sculpted out of white limestone and burnished to a golden patina. Many of the buildings, churches, duomos, campaniles, and government offices in Lecce, known as the "Florence of the South," were sculpted out of the soft local limestone. In *barocco leccese* or the Baroque-style of Lecce, the ornate architecture was characterized by the distinctive flourishes, foliated or geometric motifs, and highly sculpted figures. Sometimes the richly ornamented style (of San Giovanni Battista and the Church of St. Croce) was exuberant, with intricate flourishes resembling animals, grotesques, figures, or plants, using the finest artistic touches as on a wedding cake. Others were more sedate, like the Duomo, which held the more sculpted swirls in check.

After wandering through the churches, a twelfth century fortress, and one of the Roman amphitheaters, it was way past pranza—lunch time. We looked for a trattoria, but at first had little luck. The streets were empty of townspeople. They had to be eating somewhere. But, where? One of the few cars that passed by as we were ambling along the narrow, cobbled streets pulled near us and stopped. A man quickly hopped out of the car and began unloading cases of wine from the back of his car and hauled them into the nearest building.

"Trattoria?" I chirped. "Is that a trattoria?" My eyes widened with anticipation. Not seeing any visible restaurant signs, I followed the man into a long room with a low-vaulted ceiling—yes, it was a restaurant! I waved to Win to follow me—he is shy about going in, uninvited—and we were greeted cordially, quickly seated, and treated to a most incredible birthday feast. (Isn't that the way?)

Win ordered a plate of delicate *capocollo*, thin local ham served with fresh *melone* (cantaloupe). I had the most scrumptious *involtini di melanzane* ever: lightly fried slices of eggplant stuffed with seasoned ricotta cheese and smoked mozzarella, rolled up and smothered with tomato sauce, and baked until the mozzarella cheese oozes all over your plate. Once served, it was topped with a sprig of fresh basil. Divine! And that was just the primi course. The next course was equally delicious. We shared *spiedo martinese*, skewers of lamb, goat and veal sausages which were simply succulent and resonant of the nearby Arabic influences. Of course, we ordered a bottle of *Bombino Bianco*, a lovely white wine for the birthday boy.

Then, we dove into Winston's favorite food of all time: immense bowls of *spaghetti con le cozze*. Yes, it was just spaghetti—nothing fancier, but was house-made and delicious—plus, the mussels were swimming in a delectable saffron sauce. And the mussels were left in their shells as God intended. (Yes, we were slurping out all the briny essence.)

After our lengthy pranzo, we headed back to the car and drove a short distance to Otranto, skirted around it, and proceeded to follow the highway along the Adriatic coast south and west all along the heel of the boot, known as the Salento. This was the southernmost point of Italy's heel, and the junction of the Adriatic and Ionian Seas.

We drove past many seaside villages, saw signs for *termes*, beaches, *torres*, and *grottos*, but continued. (If we had known better, we would have stopped, as many of the grottos were over five thousand years old. It pays to have a travel guide with you.)

Stopping for a cappuccino at Santa Maria di Léuca, we found an extraordinary lighthouse over 141 feet high and 102 feet above sea level. It was said to be the second most important lighthouse in all of Italy, next to one in Genova.

At the base of the lighthouse was a basilica known as De Finibus Terre, or The End of the Land, that had been Greek at one time. It had also been commemorated to St. Peter in honor of his passage to Rome.

On a small sign we read of a legend about a beautiful white (*leukos*, in Greek) mermaid who had resided there. She was known to entice farmers and sailors alike to come to her. Strangely enough, this was also the place where the Virgin Mary saved many boats from a storm, thus the name Santa Maria di Léuca. It was like hitting the motherlode.

"Must have been quite a happening place," my husband said with a twinkle in his eye. I nodded.

The town wrapped around a small bay with sailboats bobbing below us on the deep blue waters. A few clouds rose overhead, and the sun momentarily was cast aside in a luminescent glow. From where we stood, it was an extraordinary view—this spot was the closest place to Greece in all of Italy. I couldn't help but gaze out to the Mediterranean and marvel at all that had transpired on this one little spot on the globe.

Before the sun began its slide into the sea, we drove along the heel of this Italian boot. We caught glimpses of the remnants of the marauding troops from centuries past, sprinkled along the shoreline like forgotten Legos or Tinker Toys: somber, tall square Norman torres that had presided over this seascape since before the fifteenth century; and the less prominent *trullis,* which are the small stone beehive-shaped shelters or hovels from the fourteenth century—all littered across open fields as we drove back to Porto Casareo. We knew a bit about these Apulian stone huts, as we had seen flyers at the hotel. We hoped to check them out in a day or so.

Tired, but a little hungry, and it was already eight o'clock, we wandered back into the little restaurant at Torre Inserraglio for a fine birthday repast of thin pizzas baked in a wood fireplace. It had been a good and very full day!

CHAPTER SIXTEEN
Porto Caesareo and Beyond

*T*he day after Winston's birthday was one of rest and relaxation—time at the beach, at the resort's beautiful pool, while reading, reading, reading. Dinner was at home—a bit of Apulia on a plate: *orecchiette con cime di rapa* (orecchiette pasta, which means "little ears," splashed with shimmering golden olive oil, garlic, dried chili flakes, broccoli rabe, and plenty of freshly grated pecorino romano.) As we ate on our balcony, we enjoyed the setting sun over the sea, and the olive groves just below us. Yes, we had a glass or two of local wine.

One day at home was lovely, but there was still so much to see. So, on the following morning, out the door we went. We soon realized we had been much too quick to judge this area. What had appeared as stark, tired, rocky soil was a place of great growth and resplendent crops. The harvesting of olives was upon us, and the fields we passed that morning were being gleaned of all kinds of produce. (What were we thinking?) With guidance at the hotel from our English-speaking concierge, Emilio, we were able to get directions to Gallipoli and to learn how to tackle necessary changes for the following week's train reservations.

We headed south to Gallipoli, a coastal town located on the

Ionian Sea, on the west coast of the Salento Peninsula. Gallipoli is a very old city, but is divided into two parts, the modern and the old. The new part of the town includes all the newest buildings including a skyscraper. And that is where we were able to quickly handle our transportation issues.

Next, like the sea-loving lemmings that we are, we headed toward the sea—the Ionian Sea. We crossed a sixteenth century bridge that connected us to a small island that was the oldest part of the city and its ancient seaport. Almost completely surrounded by fortress walls dating back to the thirteenth century, Gallipoli, meaning "beautiful city," is charming and exotic. Legend has it that this strategic location, which includes Porto Cesareo, became an early part of Magna Graecia (Greater Greece) and remained so until 265 BC, when the Greek king Pyrrhus, presumably after one too many disastrous victories, was defeated by the Romans. Yes, the city was frequently under siege—hordes of Vandals, then Goths—but once the Byzantines (predominantly Greek-speaking Romans from Constantinople during the Middle Ages) entered, the town was rebuilt and remains much in the style and architecture we saw of that time.

We parked the car near the bridge, and as we were walking on the quay toward the old town, we saw below us a small contingent of colorful fishing boats with fishermen hawking their bounty. As we walked closer, a swarthy-looking fisherman approached us, smelling much like—well, fish—holding what looked like a couple of small black balls of spines. We had no idea what he was saying, but he beckoned us toward his boat, where he cracked open a live sea urchin—yes, that's what he was holding. He pulled a miniature pink plastic spoon from his pocket and proceeded to feed us directly from the innards of this little crustacean. Like a mother bird feeding her young, he hovered over us, lovingly spooning an incredibly creamy, fresh, yet salty delicacy of light orange-colored strips into our waiting mouths. We stepped back and swallowed; we had never tasted anything quite like it, and we didn't know how to thank him. Were we to purchase a bunch of them? And put them where? How would they keep fresh? Would they keep in the back seat of a hot car? We offered payment for what we had eaten, but he just slapped Win on the back, grinned a toothless smile, and walked on to the next group of tourists coming down the steps.

We were oddly charmed. We felt somehow welcomed by this simple gesture—like receiving communion, along with a blessing—and as we continued down the quay, we moved with a different bounce in our step. So, now that we had been accepted, or made the grade, so to speak, we could begin our tour of the old town with renewed vigor and expectation.

Of course, we arrived just as most locals were preparing for pranzo. Our timing was truly lacking. We ended up following a stream of villagers down through the labyrinthine cobbled streets, where we veered off slightly, just as they turned to enter their homes. No, we were not asked in, but wouldn't that have been a treat? I stopped to take note of the variety of architecture. The Byzantine style with its Arabesque loveliness graced many of the small homes. Historical and cultural influences stood proudly on display. It was good we took note as the museums were not open—for display. One museum we were hoping to find was A Mesciu Veli, a museum in an underground olive pressing mill from the sixteenth century. We had heard that this mill had provided lighting oil—or lamp oil—for much of Europe for centuries. Ah, well. Another time.

After wandering the alleys toward the ancient castle and back again, we spotted a seafood restaurant, or *pescheria*, on a little spit of land on the opposite side of the quay. Lucky us! We were able to indulge in the freshest seafood imaginable. No, we never miss a meal, or the opportunity to try something new. Even, when we have no earthly idea what we are eating. In this case, we did. We ate raw oysters on the half shell and lightly fried calamari followed by a dish of succulent grilled shrimp, the size of small lobsters, swathed in a saffron sauce with cavatelli pasta. No need for dinner that night. And, yes, a local white wine. Does Bombino Bianco, ring a bell?

The next day, after relaxing at the pool, my husband and I opted to go on a late-afternoon English-speaking tour organized by our hotel, Torre Inserraglio. The name of the tour, A Visit to Ancient Farmhouses, was intriguing enough, but we figured we could also use some "real" English translations for a change. (We had gotten into the lazy habit of assuming we understood what was going on most of the time.)

While the bus sat idling in front of the hotel, about twenty passengers began to file inside the bus. The concierge, Emilio, had changed hats and became our tour guide. Within moments, we learned that our traveling companions were from the UK, some from Australia and Canada, but most, however, were from the US. Fortunately, all spoke English. Good. We were ready to go. Yet we continued to sit and wait.

After about twenty minutes more, Emilio mumbled something to the driver before he jumped off the bus to race back into the hotel. He returned with two vampish-looking gals in tow. The two were dressed for . . . well, not for walking around a farm. Leopard-skin tights, high-heeled slings, low-cut peasant blouses . . . and was that a flask they were carrying?

"From LA," they tossed down the aisle, as a full and complete excuse for their tardiness. Los Angeles!

"Figures," I heard someone behind us mumble. I found myself nodding. No other explanation was offered for keeping an entire busload waiting. The two women simply giggled, threw back their hair, and from that point presided over the tour as if they were our designated guides.

The bus pulled out of the hotel parking lot and traveled away from the coast heading south and deeper into the interior of the peninsula. Craggy beaches and scrappy plots of land gave way to fields yielding a variety of crops: grapes, olives, wheat, voluptuous tomatoes, melons, and eggplant. We were told this area cultivates a special red grape, known as Negroamaro, for a wine brought to Puglia by Illyrian colonists before the Greeks arrived in the seventh century BC.

"Horace and other Roman writers have mentioned *mera tarantina* from Taranto, and Pliny the Elder described Manduria, a city north of Porto Caesareo, as a *'viticolosa,'* or full of vineyards during his time," Emilio continued. "The Negroamaro grape may have been brought by traders from the homes of winemakers in Asia Minor at any point in the last eight thousand years." Emilio stated all of this eloquently through a static-encumbered radio. Unfortunately, the radio was not the only static, as the tartelettes from LA were also waxing poetic. We slid down in our seats attempting to ignore them. We pretended we were not from the US and did not tell anyone we were from California.

"From this day forward," we whispered to each other, "we will say we are from Canada." We prayed no one from Canada would press us for details and we continued to ignore the two ladies up front.

Since the tour had promised a wine tasting shortly—which we were now truly looking forward to—we tried to enjoy ourselves as we bounced along rutted farm roads to the first of several *masserie,* or ancient farmhouses.

I must admit, the farmhouses were not what I expected. I grew up in the Midwest, so I thought I knew what an ancient farmhouse looked like. I may have been expecting early nineteenth century scenes as in the "American Gothic" painting by Grant Wood. But these were not ordinary houses. In fact, they were not houses at all. They were large, abandoned stone enclosures—*castelli*—or castles, which had been built possibly as early as the thirteenth and fourteenth centuries. Or was it the seventeenth century? (Some understanding was lost as we all piled off the bus.)

The first and most impressive of the masserie had very thick stone walls, probably thirty feet tall with crenellated towers at the corners. A ten-inch-thick wooden gate was the doorway into a courtyard/farmyard. High above the wooden gate were stone chutes which served to deliver boiling hot (olive) oil onto unsuspecting and unwanted marauders. *Egad! Is that really a good use for olive oil?*

Pushing the heavy gate open, Emilio led us into the courtyard, which was open to the elements above, much like a classically designed hacienda. Along one of the inner walls was an uneven set of stone steps that led to the upper chambers above. Extremely dilapidated antique trunks, broken mirrors, picture frames, and furniture remained from ages past, all scattered around the chamber floors, now covered in dust, bird dung, and mice droppings.

"What happened to these people? Where did they go in such a hurry?" I asked.

"I believe these messerie or castellos were abandoned after World War II as the owners either could not be found or could not pay back taxes and never returned."

"But who lived here in the first place?" asked someone from the back of our tour group.

"I'm glad you asked," Emilio said, as he led us from one room to another. "These farmhouses were once homes to lords and ladies, who had *contadini* (peasants) living outside the gates to care for them, along with the fields, vineyards, and olive orchards. But when the pillaging hordes descended from the seas and the pirates raced inland, the peasants and animals were brought inside these enclosures for the masters' protection. Overtime, the peasants could own a small parcel of land to farm, and then the owners were somewhat on their own."

"Like in Poderi," I whispered to Winston. He nodded but shushed me into silence.

We all took turns peering out the cracked and filthy castle windows to the fields beyond. The silvery-gray leaves of the olive trees bent with a gentle but hot breeze. Inside those thick walls, the dank rooms remained cool.

"All is quiet now," Emilio said softly, as if preparing us for some secret event, "but soon there will be the unforgettable sound of the whack, whack, whacking of the branches as the ripened olives are stripped from the olive trees."

"Sounds like near Poderi," I said to Win. "Exactly," he whispered back.

". . . And once the olive presses begin," Emilio continued, "barrel upon barrel will be filled with that luxuriant of all golden liquids, the life-giving secret of the Mediterranean, our fine olive oil."

"I'm not certain pouring boiling oil on marauding hordes is how I would use the olive oil," someone said. A slight titter ensued.

"But, if that's the only deterrent," someone else chimed in.

"More like life-taking," said another.

Emilio smiled and continued. "And, down that road," he said, pointing through the cracked pane of glass, "the wheat fields have recently been harvested, providing the grain or semolina for producing our precious pasta. Apulia is known as the breadbasket of Italy and produces 80 percent of all Europe's pasta. And along with our abundant wine and hand-crafted cheeses, all the products that come from this area round out the needs for all humanity!"

He pulled his hand back from the window, shifted his dusty sunglasses further up his nose, and led us back down the stairs. Ahead of us, mice scurried out of our way to resume their jobs as lone caretakers of this abandoned castle.

We visited several other abandoned farmhouses, identical in their disrepair, and then made our way to a working farm where we were introduced to the flavors of sheep's cheese, fresh grapes, and homemade sausages. Emilio, by that point having either sipped some wine on the side or taken a swig from the LA gals' flask, was encouraging us to come behind the barn and into a fenced paddock where an enormous bull was pawing the ground. The lovely Miss LaLas immediately took him up on the offer and pranced through the gate, their sling-back heels sinking down into the . . . when suddenly, the owner lurched into the paddock and whisked the women and Emilio out of harm's way. He spoke in rapid Italian to Emilio, who turned red, apologized, and herded us all hastily back into the shuttle. *Olé!*

As we were heading to our next destination—the vineyard for wine tasting—we passed by a truck being loaded with melons—cantaloupes—and the LA gals screamed for the bus to stop. Emilio had the driver slam on the brakes and the gals hopped off. Emilio followed. He had no idea what they were up to, but we could tell he was enamored with this colorful duo. He tumbled off the bus behind them. As we observed from inside the bus, the melon growers, wearing cheerful smiles, were quickly accommodating a request from Emilio. Machetes and knives were pulled out from the truck bed. A fellow tourist from behind us screamed, and all eyes quickly focused on the movement of a steel blade. It was raised overhead and with a flash crashed down and through a melon. In no time at all, we were all off the bus sampling the most delicious, sweet, succulent melon I believe I have ever tasted. Like no other melon! Is that possible? Well, we would give the gals from LA this one. It was a decadent treat to sample! And under memorable circumstances.

But wait! Did the Lolitas pay the melon growers? No, they just climbed back on the bus and began yelling, "Get thee to the winery! Get thee to the winery!" Before I boarded, I turned to face the exuberant and gregarious melon growers. Disbelief filled their large brown eyes. Did I detect disappointment? Now I was feeling really embarrassed. And I wasn't the only one. Without a word being muttered among us tourists, wads of lira were quietly stuffed into the large paw of one of the farmer's open hands. We all hopped back on the bus and off to the winery. A stilted silence replaced the earlier jubilant mood.

Well, I don't know if the winery was expecting our little entourage, but a formal wedding party was in full swing when we arrived. People in formal attire—young, middle-aged, babies, and old duffers—were enjoying a warm afternoon of celebration and revelry. No telling how long the drinking had been going on. But despite arriving in our finest ancient farm-stomping duds, we were welcomed with goblets—not tiny paper cups or *piccolo* (little) glasses—but goblets filled to the brim with the deep dark wine we had been told of earlier—negroamaro. A lusty, full-bodied red with an intense and heady aroma. And another salice salentino, which was a chardonnay-based white wine with a fruity whiff was also served. With dust in our hair and teeth, we wiped our hands on our pant legs, licked our lips clean, and sampled—gulped down—a goblet of each. We were finally getting into the party mood.

By the time we entered the city gates of Nardò an hour later, we all were feeling no pain. Where some had started earlier in the afternoon, we all quickly caught up. It was after seven o'clock in the evening when we arrived and we probably could have used some more food, as the few samplings of meat and cheese—how long ago was that?—had become a dim memory.

Emilio mentioned in passing that he had never led this tour before. All of us patrons were clear on that point but were willing to give him the benefit of the doubt. "Oh, you are doing such a great job!" We were hoping for sustenance at that point. But instead of finding food, he walked us down the cobblestone streets *en groupe* through the lovely Baroque town and toward the town square, Piazza Salandra. Like Lecce, this was an unbelievably beautiful city, also filled with Baroque monuments and churches. But before we could get our bearings, Emilio led us directly into the massive city hall and its immense meeting chamber.

"This is where our mayor and the members of his council hold their meetings," he said with a wave of his hand. "I've made arrangements with the mayor and he is awaiting our arrival. I'll go find him."

While Emilio was gone, we could sit in the council members' seats awaiting the mayor's arrival. We waited. And waited some more. We needed food. The hall was hot and stifling. Windows, twenty-five feet above us, were calling to us to open them, but, of course, we couldn't.

The LA contingent, not to sit without merriment, made their way to the imposing high court desk where the mayor of the city obviously conducted his business. They took turns swiveling round and around in the mayor's seat, banging the gavel, and calling us to order. They continued their antics to the point we were sobering up and we wanted out. Finally, as we stood to leave the hall, the mayor came in with Emilio and was introduced to our group. The mayor, like all good ambassadors (politicians), made light of the antics of the gals who continued to swivel in his seat as he took their behavior in stride. (Of course, their flirtatious methods probably endeared them to him.) We were lucky to be able to hear his warmhearted welcome to Nardò, along with a bit of the city's history. But my ears were burning with embarrassment because of those two "ugly Americans." Or maybe I wasn't sober enough, but I wanted to leave. Finally, the mayor led us back outside into the town square where the air had become much cooler. And he invited us to the evening's festa, which was being set up at that very moment.

Colored lights were being strung across the square and being looped back and forth across the streets, connecting from the center monument to the store fronts and back again. Men of all ages, standing or sitting near the square, were chatting, smoking, or drinking coffee, while patiently waiting. To the side, a band was being set up on a small stage and musicians were warming up for the occasion. "Come back in thirty minutes or so and we'll be ready for you," the mayor said, waving his hand over his shoulder and promising a dance or two with the gals.

Emilio led us back down the street and through the side doors of one after the other beautiful Baroque cathedrals, basilicas, or churches, to the point that everything was beginning to blur. Unfortunately our timing was off, as a service was going on in each location. Yet Emilio carried on in a rather loud voice, pointing out the history and artifacts of each wondrous church. I felt squeamish at our intrusion. The pews were filled with elderly women, no men, all dressed in black, with black scarves tied under their chins, kneeling and praying in a most reverential fashion—but definitely aware of our intrusion and sending the most malevolent glowers our way.

Emilio continued. Win and I slid out a side door hoping the group would follow in short order, and we wouldn't be left behind. But then, would that have been so bad? When the group finally appeared, we made our way back to the festa where the music was getting into full swing.

When I looked around the crowd, I noticed there were no women, just men. But then I noticed a young, voluptuous woman in a tight red dress, long, dark hair cascading down her back, strolling into the square on the arm of a man three times her age. Definitely not her grandfather, and the men began crowding around her.

"Where are all the women?" I whispered to Emilio. "Who are these men going to dance with?"

Emilio looked at the crowd, then back at me in surprise. "You already saw them, Signora! They are busy praying for their men back in those churches!"

"All of them?" I asked again, in disbelief.

"Oh, my, yes! Once a woman is married, she rarely returns to the festas."

"Do they always wear black?" someone else asked.

"Oh, but they do. They wear black for all those who have died."

"But were all of them widows?"

"Oh, no, no, signoras," Emilio said matter-of-factly. "Once a woman is married, surely there will be a time when someone she knows dies, so it is understood that she, as a woman, must spend her time praying for their souls."

I gulped and grabbed my throat. I felt like I was choking. I couldn't imagine living under such circumstances and strictures. At that point, the women from LA began sauntering toward the center of the festa. They were in search of the mayor who had promised them a dance. Unfortunately for them, our tour bus pulled up, beeped the horn, and before we could experience one moment of the festa, or partake in some street food, we were carted back to the safety of the hotel. Hungry, but totally relieved to be home. *Are there any leftovers in the fridge?*

Lazio

CHAPTER SEVENTEEN
All Roads Eventually Lead to Rome

We left early the following morning for Brindisi to catch a train to Rome. We were quite excited about taking the luxurious nonstop Eurostar, especially after our previous gear-shifting, black-smoke belching experience from Salerno. This excursion promised to be glorious, although we were a bit nervous about navigating the big city of Rome. We arrived at ten-thirty for our noontime train. Waiting on the platform, I asked Win, "Which way is north?" (I am always wanting to know the points of the compass—always needing to know which direction we're heading. I suppose it comes from growing up in the middle of a very flat state (Nebraska) where knowing my bearings was an imperative.)

"Why do you ask?" he said, and began looking up and down the tracks. The sun was overhead, so it was difficult to tell.

"Because that's the direction we will be heading to Rome. If we're in the first-class section, car 3, then we need to be standing closest to north, to be near the front of the train, right? That way we won't be forced to run the entire length with our bags." Specters of past moments of lost sanity catching a train flitted through my mind.

"North is that way," I heard a voice boomed out in English

from a nearby bench. Two young men stood up, introduced themselves as John and Tim, and we struck up a conversation. They, too, had been traveling throughout Italy, and we shared similar stories. Of course, when we found out they were from LA, we didn't share the previous night's story about the drama queens. We could tell the two men were cut from a better quality of cloth. In fact, they each wore fine leather jackets draped over their shoulders. Certainly, a find from Florence.

When we discovered we would all to be in the same car in first class, we stood together where we determined the train would stop and we could easily step on. (John and Tim had faced this conundrum before, as well. We laughed. Hasn't everyone?) The twelve o'clock Eurostar arrived promptly at 1:15. We sighed with relief and waited for it to come to a full stop. Announcements in Italian indicated that because of the late arrival, the train would make only a brief stop, so—*essere pronto a tutto* (hurry, hurry, hurry) and be prepared for anything.

The exceedingly long train took an incredibly long time to come to a full stop. Instantly, the narrow platform became an enormous swarm of people pushing and shoving to get on or off. Passengers staggered with their luggage to go in any and all directions. At the same time, the four of us tried to avoid falling onto the tracks.

Suddenly it became apparent that despite our preparation and scientific analysis of north and south-going cogitations, we were, indeed, at the wrong end of this long train. We grabbed up our months' worth of bags and began to run to the opposite end. Shortly, we heard the conductor blowing his whistle and over the crowd saw him waving wildly for us to get onboard. Clearly, the train was going to leave—with or without us. As panic set in, Win made a hasty decision and heaved his bags into the closest door. John and Tim followed suit and leaped aboard behind him. That left me on the platform, huffing and puffing to catch up, then swinging my heavily laden bags through the closest door available. As one of our new-found friends turned to help me, I caught sight of my husband disappearing into the next car.

I'm on my own! The thought terrified me.

It was now clear I needed to move my two bags—with John's help—ten cars forward. Ten cars? Yes. The train began to roll and within seconds had picked up enough speed to propel us side to side as we tried to keep our balance. Tim had followed Winston and, fortunately, John stayed with me, assisting me to get from one car to another. We squeezed down each aisle, trying not to bump into everyone en route, and sidled through the pneumatic doors between the cars. We were making progress.

"Where on earth did they go?" I whimpered, knowing John had no more idea than I did. *Does Winston even know if I made the train?* Sweat was dripping down my face and beginning to burn my eyes. Win and Tim were still missing in action.

Three cars forward, we entered the dining car. "I believe we are in for a challenge," John said to me. I gulped. I'm sure he was sorry he had been the last to leap on the train before me. But he smiled kindly. A serving cart obstructed the entire aisle, and we realized we would need to lift each of our four pieces of luggage over the heads plus over the serving cart without knocking carafes of coffee or bottles of wine onto the floor. With pure frenzy and desperation on my part, I heaved each bag to John, who lifted them over and down into the aisle on the other side of the cart. Whew!

We were making good progress and were about to enter the second to the last car where our seats were waiting, when the pneumatic doors once again snicked open. Suddenly, John's beautiful leather jacket—the one he had so elegantly draped over his shoulder—was sucked in between the door and the door casing. With that, the door would neither open nor close, as that gorgeous jacket had made a wedge of itself that blocked the door from operating. With perspiration pouring down our faces, we tugged and pulled on that coat, stretching the coat beyond recognition. Finally, it became dislodged from what could have been its final resting place.

At least ten long minutes later—from the moment of leaping onto the train and making our way to our seats—John and I finally found Tim and Win casually relaxing in their seats. (*Maybe it wasn't that long—or maybe longer! Who's to say?*)

"We're just holding your seats for you," they muttered lamely. I collapsed into mine. Blessedly, I couldn't speak.

"So, how about I buy you all a drink in the dining car?" Winston suggested with a lightness I'm sure he didn't feel. "I owe you one!" Oh, did he ever, and more than just one.

I hadn't yet caught my breath, and the thought of facing the same crowd in the dining car that John and I had just lurched through, handing our luggage overhead and cart, seemed all too soon. But a free drink is a free drink. Plus, the dining car was not all that far. I stowed my bags and after swabbing the perspiration off my face and neck, I followed them back down the aisle.

Marvelous is only one descriptor for the dining car. *Funny, I didn't pay much attention on my first pass through.* The car was beautifully appointed with luxurious blue suede seats, white tablecloths, and crystal stemware, which accompanied a delicious three-course pranzo along with excellent wines. I relaxed back in my seat and spent the next three-plus hours swilling down glasses of wine and comfortably taking note of the breathtaking mountain scenery of the Apennines as it flitted past our car—from the Adriatic to the Tyrrhenian Sea.

Rome was bustling when we arrived around five o'clock. We dragged our bags off the train, through the Termini, and up the steps, then bumped down three blocks to Hotel Genova. We were exhausted, or intoxicated, or both. I needed a bath and a nap. Thankfully, the room was large and comfortable, the hotel was clean, and the staff was friendly and helpful. It was a lovely surprise and not exactly what we expected from this known-to-be-over-crowded tourist city. After we napped and cleaned up, we made our way down to the concierge for recommendations for a nearby restaurant. The concierge took my hand and led us out the front door and across the street to the lovely Restaurante Smeraldo, where we were introduced to the owner.

In no time at all, we settled in for our first Roman meal at a perfect outside table. As flutes of prosecco were delivered, troubadours with concertinas began hovering around. *When the moon hits your eye like a big pizza pie! That's a-mor-e!* The day's dust and anxiety slowly drifted away.

I had read up on the Roman *cucina,* which had been described as "pastoral." Well-known for lamb and pork, and for pecorino cheeses (sheep's milk cheese)—animals that graze Plus, fresh vegetables and lusty, rich pasta sauces. I began with *carciofi all giudea,* golden-fried artichokes, and Win with *suppli al telefono,* deep-fried rice and mozzarella balls. These dishes were followed by *fettuccine alla papalina* made with eggs, prosciutto, and peas—another favorite of Win's, while I had the spicy pasta, *penne all'arrabbiata.* We finished with a shared platter of *abbacchio al forno,* oven-roasted lamb with garlic and rosemary. We were not familiar with Roman wines because they lean mainly to white. So, if you want a red, order a bottle of chianti or our favorite Tuscan wine, Morellino di Scansano.

I mentioned earlier that we had not been looking forward to spending the last three days of our vacation in Rome. After spending so much time in the Italian back country, we weren't certain we would have the stomach or fortitude for the onslaught of humanity. We expected Rome to be noisy, dirty, and unfriendly. But we were in for a marvelous new experience! Yes, we joined the crowds of people who have come to love Rome. That evening, many at adjoining tables—from Sweden, Australia, the UK and the US—enlightened us about the wonders we could look forward to. Ideas were shared for places to visit, places to avoid, gifts to buy, and we all felt one with the world. And because we were within crawling distance of our beds, we accepted the "house specialty" and our favorite *digestivo*: limoncello. Rome took on an otherworldly glow!

CHAPTER EIGHTEEN
Veni, Vidi, Vici – I Came, I Saw, I Conquered

*A*t last, my eighth grade Latin class finally paid off: *Veni, vidi, vici.* I came, I saw, I conquered. And that was what we intended to do now that we were finally in Rome. *Carpé diem,* or seize the day, and all that. I suppose it makes perfect sense to reflect on those words, since it was Horace, the Roman poet, who coined that phrase which means "one should enjoy life while they can." And we were ready.

So, on our first full day in Rome, equipped with a trusty travel guide in tow, we headed out the door at a fast clip. We had plenty of places to see and much to do. The morning was crisp, the air surprisingly clean and refreshing, and we were excited about seeing the Roman Empire at its best. After zipping back to the Termini, the central transportation hub, we purchased tickets for the Metro and made our way to a stop at the Colosseum. We opted for self-tours for a change. Neither of us could face traipsing behind another tour guide or a raised umbrella. We wanted flexibility and to be able to take our time as we went along. With guidebook in hand, we crossed the street to begin our tour.

The immense Arch of Constantine is the largest of the three surviving Roman triumphal arches, standing 25 meters, or 75 feet, and dating to 315 AD. It was constructed in honor of Constantine's victory over his rival Maxentius. But this victory, and therefore this arch, was significant because it was the premise for granting freedom of worship to Christians and the first step toward the empire's Christianization (the Edict of Milan in 313 AD). The decorative sculpture (bas relief) on all faces of this enormous edifice tells the story of the six episodes of wars fought with Maxentius. Ironically, Roman pagan gods and goddesses cavort across and around this arch, despite the fact that it represents giving up the gods for the one true Christian god.

Next, we wandered across the street and through the ancient Forum, which served as the marketplace. The Forum, which was the heart of ancient Rome and center of daily life, housed several important buildings, temples, statues, and monuments. One of the most important buildings was the Roman Senate, where elections, public speeches, and trials were handled. We made our way to that building, where we thought of our dear friend, Cicero. (This lawyer and statesman had become a real hero of ours in our Roman studies.) We stepped onto one of the three broad steps where, at one time, three hundred senators wou . have been seated. What elegant discourses reverberated through this massive but austere hall? What words of encouragement or discord were given to fellow Romans? What rash decisions were uttered by Julius Caesar? What wars did Caesar Augustus declare here? What arguments did Cicero put forth in this space? I looked around me, listening. I felt I could hear the past.

The hall was spartan, at best (which, as I think of it, is a Greek term, and not Roman), but all I could think of was a quote from Cicero: "A room without books is like a body without a soul." Well, of course, there were no books left behind. The beautifully carved interior walls had been stripped of frescoes and wall hangings long ago. There are hallowed halls, but this felt more like a hollow hall. We left the Senate wanting to know so much more.

We made our way across the street, where we climbed up many stairs and ramps inside the Colosseum. We were smart this time (memories of being herded through Pompeii were still fresh) and we rented audio tours. After plugging into the system, we staggered from one point of interest in history to another.

The Colosseum, built between 75 AD and 80 AD, is an immense elliptical space which rises 161 feet high, and is divided into three main floors with eighty arches. Although the events which were held in this enormous amphitheater were free, special preferential seating was given to the imperial section, magistrates, and senators. Special passageways were even designed for the emperor and his party and for the Vestal Virgins to pass through, so as not to commingle with the "mongering hordes."

The lowest seating section (*cavea*) was for the knights, the middle section for the middle class, and the third cavea for the general public—not so different from today's stadiums and amphitheaters. There were fifty rows of seats built of stone—for the imperial audience—and for the plebian section, seats of wood.

We climbed up to the third level (where we plebeians belonged) and sat in the stadium seats to take in the overall view of the arena. I was trying to imagine what the long-ago experience must have been like. I've seen movies and heard tales of slaughtered Christians, but to sit here in person was more daunting than I expected. Below us, where a floor had once stretched across the ground, only supporting infrastructure, known as the *hypogeum*, remained. As if having been flayed open, the gaping corridors below revealed the gladiators' quarters and tunnels and where wild animals had been held in cages. Our audio guide explained that the cages were raised and lowered by a special pulley system, and that mechanical systems opened causeways to flood the arena for naval battles. It was simply too awesome to imagine.

The guide also described another mastery of engineering—a complex series of corbels in the attic that supported an enormous awning. Made of silk and linen, this awning protected the interior of the arena from the elements, covering a surface area of 22,000 square meters. We looked up at the sky, imagining the awning of two thousand years before and how it had shielded the attendees. Large cumulus clouds were beginning to form and darken over us.

"I believe the word 'cumulus' is from the Latin word '*cumulo*,' meaning heap or pile," I said, sounding astute. (Yes, my eighth grade Latin was coming in handy.) "I wonder if the word was invented while sitting in this arena. Ah, tut, tut, it looks like rain. Let's pull up the awning now."

"Possibly. But its cumulonimbus clouds that produce rain," Win said with a shrug. (His forte may not have been Latin, but it was strong in math and sciences.)

We wandered up and down and around the complex and investigated as much as we were allowed. Time passed quickly. We were fascinated with the history, architecture, the engineering feats, and so much more. We tried to imagine life and death that had taken place in this spot in the first century.

Suddenly, those cumulous clouds turned into dark, foreboding—yes, cumulonimbus—clouds moving in from the Tyrrhenian Sea. We decided this was a good time to take our leave, as we were hungry. And, of course, we had forgotten our umbrella. We raced down the steps and across the street to what looked like a wonderful outdoor restaurant. Ristorante Massenzio's broad canvas umbrellas covered the outdoor patio and would protect patrons from the rain. At that moment, a dappled bit of sunlight still danced in and out from above. The atmosphere was festive, with laughter, music, the hum of chatter, and the pop of wine corks all growing louder as we entered. We noticed right away what people were eating: the *specialita pesce fresco* (fresh seafood specialties). Enormous bowls—troughs, some might say—were filled with mountains of *cozze* (mussels) and *vongole* (clams) swimming in a tantalizingly aromatic wine broth. The scent of garlic and fresh herbs hovered above us and around us. Of course, we had no choice. We had to order a bowl of each. With a bottle of pinot grigio and a basket of bread, we dug in. And dug. And ate. Those bowls, it seemed, were bottomless.

And then the storm hit—with a vengeance. Not a simple sprinkle, but an all-out downpour. But what did we care? We were fully protected by the canopies—which just began to lift and waft above our heads. Slight gaps appeared between the canopies, as the elements from above began to roar. As the sail-like umbrellas sagged with rainwater, the wind, which was now blowing rain horizontally, tipped the canopies slightly. Suddenly, a deluge dumped into the laps of unsuspecting and startled diners. Screams and shrieks sounded as a mad scramble of wet folks grabbed their food and made a hasty exit into the restaurant. Those of us still gorging ourselves looked up for a slight nod, checked the umbrella above us, and went back to the job at hand. But, one by one, diners who had been certain of their safety moments earlier, and were confidently huddled under the precarious covering, ultimately became drenched too. They, too, grabbed their food, and with the help of waiters, rushed inside. In no time at all, more than thirty people had made a hasty retreat. And there we were, the only ones stalwartly left eating. Yes, our feet were soaked, but our heads and food were dry.

Finally, with the encouragement of three dripping-wet wait staff, we abandoned ship and headed inside. I don't remember much about the interior of the restaurant, but I do recall the odor of wet people, clothes, and soggy socks which seemed to rise above the briny aromas of succulent seafood. We were wedged at a small table jammed into a corner with our salvaged bowls of bivalves and glasses of wine. That was all that mattered to us, as we quietly finished our *pranzo*.

After our fine repast, and the sun had reappeared, we made our way—soggy socks and all—up the long Capitoline Hill. Once the highest of the seven hills of Rome, this had been known as the Citadel during ancient Roman times. Several significant temples had been built on Capitoline Hill, such as the temples of Juno Moneta or Virtus. But the most important was the Temple of Jupiter Optimus Maximus Capitolinus, built in 509 BC. At that time, the Hill and the Temple of Jupiter became the symbol of Rome, the capital of the world.

But as we read in our guidebook, sadly, not much remained of the temples from that era. So, it was during the Italian Renaissance—nearly two thousand years later—that Michelangelo—yes, my dear friend, Michelangelo—was commissioned by Pope Paul III to completely redesign the hilltop space. It became known as Piazza del Campidoglio. The Pope's goal was to impress Charles V, the Holy Roman Emperor, who was due to visit Rome with a unique symbol of the "new" Rome. Begun with the creation of three new or newly restored buildings, the plaza faced away from the ancient Roman Forum—the heathen Romans of yesteryear—toward the Vatican and newly refurbished Rome.

"I wonder if that decision was the Pope's or Michelangelo's?" I asked Winston. He laughed and nodded. I had read lengthy excerpts to him from my copy of *The Agony and the Ecstasy*, wherein Michelangelo had been, time and again, at odds with the various popes he worked for. Sometimes under the threat of imprisonment if he did not fulfill their wishes. Oh, the pressures of employment.

Holding the most prominent position in the oval courtyard was a statue of Roman Emperor Marcus Aurelius. This was the only bronze statue that had survived since antiquity, and the base, itself, was designed by Michelangelo. Was Mike giving the Roman gods their just due?

The elegant yet Baroque palaces, which were built on the peak of Capitoline Hill, had once been homes to the elite in the 1500s. Now, those same buildings are museums for fine art and sculpture of the most incredible of ancient beauties—all from Roman, Greek, and Egyptian eras. My favorite was a Greek bronze sculpture from the Hellenistic era, known as *Boy Removing a Thorn*. It's a common theme—a young naked lad sitting on a rock removing a thorn from his foot—supposedly, gotten from working in the vineyards. His muscles are tensed so as not to feel the pain, tendrils of his hair lay lank on his neck, and his head is bent over the throbbing foot. Such a simple act captured with such grace and elegance. A gift to behold.

Even though I was exhausted, we decided not to backtrack to the Metro, as we felt we could easily walk to our hotel. Well, it was much farther than either of us thought, but the beautiful chapels and ancient dwellings we saw along the way were worth it.

After returning to our room and my (required) nap was had, we ended up having a quiet evening and dinner at a lovely but nearby sidewalk trattoria. We fell into bed early. Roaming around Rome had taken its toll. Images of gladiators danced in my head.

CHAPTER NINETEEN
É Questa la Fine o L'Inizio?
Is This the End or the Beginning?

Mangia bene, ridi spesso, ama molto.
Eat well, laugh often, love much.

*T*he following morning, our final day in Italy, we rose quickly, as we had booked an early tour at the Vatican with a special visit to the Sistine Chapel. We were most fortunate to be able to enter the buildings before the clamoring crowds. Both Winston and I, having taken multiple classes in Renaissance art, were doubly excited to see one of Michelangelo's most famous works of art—his frescoes on the ceiling and all along the walls of the Sistine Chapel. And, we knew from my favorite source, *The Agony and the Ecstasy*, that he had painted this chapel under duress. Knowing Michelangelo's preferred art form was sculpture, Pope Julius II (known as *il papa terrible*) compelled him to paint the ceiling and walls for Pope Sixtus IV, for whom the chapel was named. To refuse would have meant prison, so Michelangelo accepted Pope Julius's request.

No matter his artistic forte, nothing could have prepared me for the exceptional beauty he captured on the walls and ceiling of the chapel; it was a room of heavenly glory. Until you witness the frescoes in person, you cannot comprehend their magnificence. And, even if you don't have a religious bone in your body, you would find it difficult to deny the power and divine qualities Michelangelo has given to God as His hand reaches out to Man in the most famous fresco, *The Creation of Adam.*

But in the chapel, all of this is sixty-eight feet above your head. Visitors are not allowed to take photos or videos, so you can't capture the majesty. The significant "kinking" of my neck eventually got the best of me.

"If I could just lie down on the floor to look up," I whimpered to Win. "I could capture all the wonder." Ah, but the crushing crowds which came coursing through the doors made that dream impossible.

Before leaving, we took time to appreciate the frescoes on the chapel walls and above the altar. On the north wall six frescoes depicting events from the life of Christ as painted by Perugino, Botticelli, Ghirlandaio, and Rosselli. On the south wall were six other frescoes depicting events from the life of Moses. And, above these works, smaller frescoes between the windows depicted various popes. It was Michelangelo's *Last Judgment* over the altar that held our interest, as we remembered the classroom discussion over the great controversy surrounding this gigantic fresco. Who was it who had upset Michelangelo during that period, only to have the artist paint the offender into the scene of hell, fire, and brimstone with a snake coiled over his nether regions?

My husband, always better with names and historical facts, said, "I believe the legend goes that Michelangelo, upset by the criticism by a Vatican dignitary by the name of Cesena, who said the mostly nude figures in the enormous work of art 'belonged in a tavern,' decided to paint this man into the bottom right hand corner."

We took a closer look at the fresco, and there in all his glory was a nude fellow, Cesena we imagined, portraying the Greek mythological god, Minos, with a serpent biting at his genitals. We giggled like school children with the carnal knowledge of this happenstance.

Once we stepped out of the Sistine Chapel and into the hallway, we made our way back to the Raphael Rooms to see one of Raphael's most famous pieces of art, *The School of Athens.* We were familiar with this grand fresco as this represented the dominant theme to the classical studies class we had taken. As a pure statement of the influence of Italian Renaissance, Raphael had chosen the theme of how Classical Greece and Rome, or pagan nations, continue to influence Christian Italy in both spiritual and worldly wisdom. (That must have been an inflammatory stand to take at the time—and in the Vatican, of all places.) The wall painting represented the classic origins of theology, law, literature, poetry, music, and philosophy. Figures representing each of the subjects that were encouraged to be mastered to hold a true philosophic debate— geometry, arithmetic, astronomy, and solid geometry—are shown in a concrete form. The main arbiters of this rule are shown in the center of the fresco—Plato and Aristotle—engaged in a dialogue. In the foreground was our dear, Michelangelo painted in by his friend, Raphael, while Michelangelo was busy next door painting the Sistine Chapel. Thus was the reverence shown for Michelangelo by a fellow artist. We loved it, and stood for as long as we were allowed, to take it all in. This very piece of art had introduced us to the magnificent world of classical art, literature, and history. We were, indeed, grateful to finally see it in person.

Next, we made our way through some of the Vatican Museums (there are fifty-four in all), which house collections of artifacts from specific eras: in the Egyptian section there were more Egyptian mummies than I had seen on display in Cairo; in the Etruscan section, we viewed finer relics than we had witnessed in Tuscany; and in the Archaeological section were ruins taken from a necropolis outside of ancient Rome, plus the remains of pre-Christian sanctuaries.

"Doesn't this make you wonder how all of these pieces of art, sculpture, and artifacts came into the hands of the Popes in the first place?" Winston whispered.

I nodded. The wealth of the Catholic Church was fully on display, and I must admit, it felt a bit unseemly. But then, who am I to judge?

We then backtracked through St. Peter's Plaza to the Basilica. To describe the interior of this massive, ornate, and masterpiece-filled center of the Christian faith is almost impossible. Throughout, the brilliance of gold radiated from both Renaissance and Baroque art. We picked up an English-only guidebook and began to make our way through this colossal and holy place.

"The original Basilica was built over the burial grounds of St. Peter during the fourth-century AD by Emperor Constantine," Winston read to me.

"Really? St. Peter was actually interred here? Makes you wonder how that happened, doesn't it?" I whispered. Surely, I was speaking heresy here, but I honestly didn't know. Having been raised as an Episcopalian, I had not thought to question this fact. The Vatican had not been the center of my world, but Christianity had been. I had only known Peter to have been a saint.

Winston leaned over to me and read from his booklet, "Peter came to Rome and spent thirty-four years as the designated head of the Christian faith. When he was crucified for his beliefs, he requested to be crucified upside down, as he felt he was not worthy to suffer the same death as Jesus Christ."

"Well, there! I guess that answers it. What else do you have about this church being built here?"

Winston continued to read, "The architectural design, at that time, was a typical basilica form, with the shape of the building being a Greek cross, a tau. Eleven hundred years later, the present Basilica was architecturally designed by Donato Bramante, from Florence." We were familiar with the genius of Bramante from our classes.

". . . About forty years later, Michelangelo was enlisted, as an artist and architect, to take over the building site at which four piers, enormous beyond any constructed since ancient Roman times, were rising behind the remaining nave of the old basilica. . . ." Win continued reading.

At the mention of Michelangelo, I tuned in. "He inherited numerous plans designed and redesigned by some of the greatest architectural and engineering minds of the 15th century, including Bramante. The plans called for a dome to equal the one engineered by Florence's Brunelleschi at the Duomo."

"That was the very dome and cathedral we had visited in Florence," I broke in excitedly. We knew it had been built a century earlier than this one in Rome, but we also knew that the dome in Florence had literally dominated the skyline of Michelangelo's childhood. Anyone who grew up in Firenze (Florence) during that one-hundred-year period of the fifteenth century awakened to the resonating sound of the stone masons busy wielding their chisels and hammers to erect that beautiful engineering marvel.

We began wandering through the massive cathedral oohing and aahing at every step. "Carlo Maderno and Gian Lorenzo Bernini," Win continued, "were also artists and architects brought in from Florence. Maderno designed the façade which is 376 ft wide and 149 ft high and was built of travertine stone.

Bernini's works included the baldachin (baldacchino), the Chapel of the Sacrament, the plan for the niches and loggias in the piers of the dome and the chair of St. Peter over the main altar." We pivoted to take in all this glory.

But nothing could have prepared me for the breathtaking beauty of the near life-sized sculpture of Michelangelo's most famous work. The Pietà, meaning "pity" or "compassion," represented Mary, who sorrowfully cradled the lifeless body of her son following crucifixion. The tenderness in this masterpiece touched my heart, filled my eyes with tears, and brought me to my knees. I wept. A mother's love has never been so exquisitely wrought.

Rising to my feet, I dabbed my eyes dry and followed Winston down the aisle. We were scheduled to take a trip to the crown, the top of the dome itself. It was quite a task. After purchasing tickets and taking an elevator to the highest point inside the Basilica, we were able to look down to the nave or gallery 450 feet below us. It was quite beautiful from every angle. We could see the magnificent altar below us, as well as marvel at the lovely Baroque artwork that lined the interior dome near us. It was thrilling. From there, we walked outside onto the roof of the first level, that is above the main church. We found a small coffee bar where we sat and had a coffee. We also took time to check out the statuary of Christ's disciples that lined the roof and overlooked St. Peter's Square. From this up-close angle, the statues were immense.

It was at this point my dear husband confided that he was not up to climbing to the cupola as planned. I believe I mumbled something like, "Why not?" The tickets had already been purchased, and I am much better at heights than he. (He says he is better at widths, so we'll go with that.) So off I went. With my usual camera hanging around my neck, Win kindly added the heavy video camera to my load, and I began my solo trek to the top. My incentive? Well, I knew Michelangelo had a hand in creating the dome, so to say I was getting a "real high" (metaphorically) on this man was to put it mildly.

I entered a stairway of sorts with dozens of other equally foolish tourists, which led us to the highest pinnacle of the Basilica. But the deal is this: as we continued to climb up the steps, we were actually walking up steps that were sandwiched between three walls—the three same walls that form the outer and inner dome. (Imagine three identically shaped upside-down bowls separated by two staircases that do not intersect. Does that help?) On top of that, I am short—only five foot two—but after a time, even I was bent over to the right to conform to the curve of the ceiling within the dome. Not sure how it all works, but I trod the steps along with others going in one direction—up. When I returned, I walked down another staircase with people only going down, and "never the twain . . . met."

I confess, it was the last five or six steps to the outside crown on the cupola that provided the most interesting challenge. A thick rope dangled from above, which I was told to grab hold of in order to haul my not-so-skinny ass up—cameras and all—to the crown, the very ledge circling the top knot of the Basilica.

I don't have a fear of heights, but if I did it might have been a wasted trip to the top, because everything was w-a-a-a-y down below. All of Rome was laid out below me like a smorgasbord. It was quite incredible to see the city from that perspective. I was able to determine which parts had been ancient Rome, what was relatively new, and what had been part of the Renaissance. For instance, the lovely Vatican gardens, which are private urban parklands that cover a vast amount of the land skirting the Vatican Museums but could only be fully viewed from the very top.

And St. Peter's Square stretched way out below me, with avenues leading out of the Square, past the city gates and to the famous Tiber River and beyond. Marvelous! And, from up there, I could wave to Winston, who had remained on the roof terrace below, and scope out where our next meal might be. I hurried down the stairs, joined my husband, went down the elevator, out of the Vatican City gates, and on to lunch. A pranzo was in order.

When in Rome, and for a light lunch, one must have pizza! (Please don't mention this to the folks in Naples, though. They don't handle this discussion well.) Just beyond the Vatican gates we found a little sidewalk eatery called Ristorante dei Musei Vaticani and ordered two medium pizzas. Mine was called *boscaiola,* or pizza with mushrooms and sausage. Win's was quite remarkable, topped with wonderful slices of bacon (prosciutto), plenty of cheese, and a fried egg. A fitting repast for weary tourists—and those who had missed breakfast and, almost, lunch. We dug in and devoured them quickly, washed down with a carafe of pinot grigio.

Next, we made our way through the streets back to the Metro. Our early morning venture had been easy, so I expected a similar return. But, at this time in late afternoon, the Metro was hot and crowded, with no seating available. And, of course, we had been forewarned about petty thieves. But, frankly, there was no way to physically move, much less abscond with anything. So, I felt perfectly safe—as long as we remembered our stop. And because all lines eventually lead back to or through Rome's Termini Station, we were good. We had only been in Rome a few days, but we knew the way. We were getting cocky!

Back in our room, we were exhausted. Yet we wanted to make our last evening in Italy memorable. After a nap (I always take one. Have you noticed?) and an invigoratingly cool shower, we sought out a restaurant which was truly Roman. As they say, "When in Rome, do as the Romans do." (Have I said this before?) So, we set off to circle the area.

The evening was still warm for late September, yet had a crisp hint of fall in the air. To our surprise, we found ourselves circling the block and returning to Restaurante Smeraldo, the place we had been introduced to on our first night. The same gallant waiter escorted us to a sidewalk table, and the same musicians came through playing concertinas. With the kind assistance of the waiter, we ordered straight from the Romana-side of the menu: olives and grilled bread for our *antipasti*, small plates of *fettuccine alla romana* and *gnocchi alla sugo* for our *primo piatto*; and *pollo alla romana* (chicken, Roman-style) and *saltimbocca* for our *secondo*. And the wine? We decided to be adventurous and tried a great bottle of white wine, known as *Est! Est! Est! di Montefiascone*—the wine so loved it was named three times: It is! It is! It is! And why not? It all adds to the ambiance, the romance.

Relaxing back in our seats, we began to play one of our favorite memory games: "What was your favorite beach, village, food, dessert, or wine of the trip?" We have always loved this game, and especially as we began to recount the historical medieval villages and grand cities we had visited over the past month. We went beyond our favorites. We listed the coastal waters we had strolled along, the seas and *termes* we had dallied in, the *tombas* we had crawled through, the museums and tours we had visited, and oh, so much more. Then we tried to name all the luscious Italian meals we had eaten, and the wines we had quaffed.

We then recalled all the fascinating and delightful people we had met along the way. Because of these newfound friends, we knew our lives would never be the same. Nor would we, as our love for each other had deepened in ways we would never have expected. There is something about finding the perfect traveling partner—because you know that you can be companions for life. This trip reaffirmed our choices.

Just then that delicious, melt-into-your-shoes-with-wonder *digestif* we had come to love was placed before us: house-made limoncello. Roman? Tuscan? Amalfitan? It mattered little, as it was pure sunshine in a thimble. Or in Italy, a glass. Here was that sweet and slightly piquant nectar from the gods. We drank to Italy; we drank to our love—and we drank to a speedy return to this marvelous country. *Salute! Cin-Cin!* To Italia!

EPILOGUE

An Embrace of Cultural Traditions

*A*bout four years later, in order to prepare for a return trip to Italy and my first trek through France with my friend Josiane (as told in Books One and Two of the *Savoring the Olde Ways* series), I contacted Lisa, who often spent her winters in San Francisco. She invited us to visit one sunny Sunday afternoon in her apartment, where we continued our conversations as if we had never stopped. Because of her wonderful gift of immersing us into the Italian culture that September four years earlier, I had taken her words to heart: Instead of just *visiting* Tuscany, I had chosen to *experience* Tuscany. I had met real people, eaten their traditional family foods, and taken part in local festivals. And I had not been the same since. But, oh, how much more I was eager to learn.

Once seated in Lisa's living room with hot tea and cookies at the ready, I began to ask more questions about the customs and traditions Winston and I had been introduced to in Poderi. Inquiring minds are always seeking more.

"To begin on a light note," I said, "I was fascinated by the *contrasto* we heard the night of the festa. We didn't understand what was going on, but it was clear it was more than singing. It was a sparring of words . . ."

"Yes, and was met with great hilarity," Winston said. "Oh, to understand a bit of Italian and be able to catch the punch line," he bemoaned.

Lisa laughed and leaned back. "I believe I actually have tapes of Algono Vinetti, a local farmer from Montemerano, who used to give a contrasto evening in Pitigliano where he would sing his poetry. It was well over twenty-five years ago, and perhaps he is no longer living. These talented men, probably our grand-fathers' ages, not only competed in the contrasto, but they also sang *la Octavina* ballads (accompanied by guitar) that they had written over their lifetimes. These were poems about the marriage of their son or the exorcism of the bad influences on the farm of a son-in-law . . ." At that point, Lisa almost jumped out of her seat.

"Oh, and there's the wonderful *moodatory,* which was wonderfully funny—serious serious—serious—but it was the talking about serious things, but with skepticism and great irony. It's an historical account of something that has happened to you but sung as a poem, like back in the '50s or '60s.

"These poems were sung about everyday events," she continued, "in an A-B-A-B fashion, but they're funny. Like the story of a new house being built, and it was being sung to the contractor. There was a wonderfully funny line like, 'You've built my house beautifully, and you've built it over—and over—and over, again; and when you come out with your calculating machine, how devilish you are at adding up all those accounts with your magical calculating machine . . .' and it goes on. And Vinetti sung it in a beautiful, resonant voice—this sixty-five or seventy-year-old man, who enjoyed singing his own poetry. And this man—this farmer—would come to town wearing a three-piece suit and a wonderful brown hat, so immaculate, so elegant. It was truly something wonderful to see and to hear."

"The contrasto certainly made a lasting impression on us," I said. "I'll never forget those wonderful, sonorous voices moving up and down the musical scales, and then the shifting into a staccato that ended with a snap. Even without understanding the words, the impact of the tempo was dramatic."

"I know what you mean," Lisa said. "I had the same impression when I first heard them, and I worked hard on my Italian to be able to pick up the thoughts behind the words, and the dialects. It was quite an undertaking, I must say." She took a sip of her tea.

"While in your home in Poderi, I remember we had some wonderful conversations about how you, a gal from San Francisco, married into an Italian family. No, a Roman family, right?" I asked.

Lisa nodded and sat up in her chair.

"I've thought about how difficult that adjustment must have been for you, and wondered if you could help me understand what it had been like?"

"Certainly. I'd be happy too."

"So, what was it like learning the customs of living in Italy and your Roman in-laws? How did you adapt to Italy as a young wife? And how do young women learn to cook even if they are raised there?"

"Let me take the last question first. The mother is always in charge of the cooking, as that is her domain," Lisa began. "So, the daughters watch. They might be allowed to prepare food at times, but it is very hierarchical. I found it very difficult to help out in other people's kitchens and actually be allowed to do things. Especially in my mother-in-law's kitchen. So you continue to watch, and perhaps you're allowed to stir something in a pan, but it's pretty much like a formal apprenticeship. This comes from their heritage, I think. So, by a certain age, you have really learned how to do certain things. Of course, some girls don't really want to learn how to cook, so they say, 'I don't want to cook,' and that's all right. It's accepted. Not everyone likes to cook. But, in Italy, usually everyone knows how to make wonderful dishes, and they have several things that are their specialties. It is such an important ability to them and is a part of good living. It is difficult not to be good at cooking certain things in that world where food is so wonderful, the vegetables are so flavorful, the cheeses are so delicious. Inspiration is everywhere around you."

She picked up her cup of tea and swirled the liquid with her spoon. "Sometimes my boys would say, 'Mom, don't come into the kitchen today because we are really hungry!' So my children, too, learned how to cook things and not necessarily complicated things. The Italian concept is that some foods go together, and some don't. And my boys really have that sense, that innate awareness.

"I learned there are rules which must be observed, of course, such as you don't put fish and cheese together—things like that. Some people know how certain wines go with certain foods, people like . . . Benino! Remember the restaurant you visited, Passaparola, in Montemerano? That was the wonderful little restaurant you gave the owner, Benino, the book, *Under the Tuscan Sun*. Benino was the one who served us the absolute best tiramisu? Benino is one of those who is so good with wines and pairing them with his food. He works a lot with the people north of Montemerano in Saturnia.

"We do remember him. And the restaurant where we had the best meal ever!" I said.

"And the best tiramisu ever!" Win said, again.

At this point, the three of us digressed into remembering the wonderful evening we had spent together at Passaparola.

"Yes, best meal ever!" I said. "I remember ordering, as my *primo piatto, acquacotta*, because you had introduced us to that wonderful traditional soup. You told us about how large oak trees were purposely left in the center of fields, so farm hands would have a nice shade tree to sit under to enjoy their daily *aquacotta* for lunch."

"That was, of course, before my time," Lisa said, "but I remember seeing some of those wonderful old photos taken during the early 1900s, where some of the people from the area, who were not allowed to own their own land at the time, were working in the fields. As I recall from one of the photos, the supervisor is seen carrying a large caldron of water, and someone else is placing onions into the pot as it is set on a fire to cook. The farm hands, during their lunch break, would eat the cooked onions and then drink the soup. That was the first aquacotta, a true peasant dish, which translates to 'water soup.' Later, when those people were given land in the 1920s and could farm on their own, they could grow their own vegetables, and then they would put chard into the soup caldron and enrich it with tomatoes. So it has a historical significance for this area. Aquacotta is a real testimony to where that culture came from."

Lisa jumped up and disappeared from the room, returning with an old photo album that showed some pictures of Poderi in the early 1900s. "When Mussolini came along and drained the swamps in the '20s," Lisa began again, "and the land slowly became arable, they developed the whole of the Manciano plain— from the sea to all the area around Poderi. In 1920, Machi Muchachi gave these people four plots of land, and if the people worked the land for twenty-five years, they would become landowners. That was when they first had the right to grow their own vegetable gardens.

"The house where I lived was built around 1868 and was built by the great-grandfather Detti. He was one of the landowners in the Poderi area, and seven of his siblings lived in those houses, which included my house. The generations from my grandparents' era had a very strong cultural link to this place, but the younger generations seem to want to move away. They look to Europe—toward tourism and sending their children abroad to get a good education. Even farmers do. They may want their children to travel to New York City or Paris to vacation or for an education, but they most often want them to go to a city to get a good job or go to university. That has been changing in the past twenty years."

Lisa went on. "But there are certain traditions still imbedded in Poderi, like the singing of the *Befana* that Margarita told you about. Do you remember that?"

We nodded with enthusiasm.

"My oldest son, Sasha, who lives in Italy, went with his wife to be in our house for the Befana this past Christmas. It was so lovely for them, because I think September 11 changed a lot of their feelings about that house. They have gone back a number of times since because it felt like a safe and quiet place to be."

"What were some of your family memories of the Befana tradition?" I asked. "It sounds so charming."

"Oh, it's quite wonderful! On the night of the 5th of January, people come from all over the province to be a part of this celebration because Poderi is one of the few remaining communities that continues to celebrate this lovely tradition. A grand crowd comes by your house with the band—a clarinet, an accordion, and a saxophone—and they sing the Befana song, which has fifteen verses. Each verse has a different meaning, and the Befana comes into your house and dances. I remember Margarita told you much of this, but all people come to take part. They go to each house in town singing this song, and the Befana comes up and dances with you and she is this little old witch who brings presents, or coal, to the children. This is because Epiphany is the next day.

"So, you are supposed to guess who the little witch is, and no one can ever guess—of course, you always know—and then the children are crying, saying 'I don't want her in my house—don't let her into my bedroom!' She wears an old rubber mask and the children want her to leave, but they also want the presents, too. You all then place a bottle of wine or some sausages into a big gunny sack as your contribution and then the sack is taken down to the school. At midnight everyone meets at the school to eat and dance. And when you all leave at the end of the evening, you sing the final Befana verse: 'We say good night, and we sing in harmony. We bring word of a great feast for tomorrow is Epiphany!' It is such a beautiful song—just beautiful!

"One time when my kids were young, we had a houseful of friends and everyone was sitting around waiting for the Befana to come down the street. People were saying, 'Oh, she's coming! My God! She's coming!' And Niccolò, my youngest son, cried, 'I don't want her to come here!' And someone took him aside and said, 'I will take care of you until she is out of here!' But, once she leaves, we all follow down the street, dancing and singing.

"Another time, we were sitting and waiting for the Befana, and our dear friends from Sweden were with us and we were all waiting. In came the Befana, and along with her was a television film crew from Channel 3 of the national television. So there we were and Niccolo was only five or six—just a little guy—and he was frightened and definitely wanting the Befana to leave. Well, the whole thing was all on television the next day—in fact, all of us were on television. Boo, our friend from Sweden, still has that video."

"We remember meeting Boo and his wife, Astrid, on the night of the festa," I said. My husband nodded.

"Speaking of tapes, I believe we still have the video tape of all of you folks dancing at the festa that September," Win said.

"In fact," I said, "we have a video of you, Lisa, dancing with the butcher from Manciano! You told us to watch for him, as he was the finest dancer in the entire province."

"Now, which one could that be?" Lisa asked "There are four brothers. First, there was Piemonte, then Imperiana, Europa, and, of course, Mondiale Giacomini."

"Mondiale was the one!" I said. "I'll never forget that name." The name rolled off my tongue like I'd become a real Italian.

"Of course. His name means 'world-famous,'" Lisa said. "As you can tell, these were great fascist names, and were from a good fascist family. They were also exceptionally good dancers."

I had no idea those names were fascist names, but yes, I could imagine they all were excellent dancers.

As memories floated through the room, we all leaned forward, simultaneously picked up a cookie apiece, and began to munch. The mystery of the "famous dancer" was solved, and we were at peace.

"Getting back to the traditions of the area," Lisa said, "I remember a book with recipes from the area of Poderi, that also tells of the traditions and includes historical stories." She drummed her chin repeatedly with the fingers of her right hand.

I practically crawled out of my chair in anticipation of seeing this cookbook.

"I wish I had a copy, as there are so many specialties," she said. My heart dropped. "There were Pina's recipes from her lovely restaurant, Cloto's recipe for aquacotta, Saturnia's recipe for aquacotta. And, of course, there is the bread from Saturnia. Most people say they won't go across the river to buy it, but they go to Saturnia all the same. I'll have to see if I can find a copy of that book for you."

"So, tell us how you began to help out at the festa when you lived there," I said.

"First of all, you were 'invited' to help. But you could not just walk in and help at just any station. No, no! I chopped salad for two years for five hours each day. Yes, you get tired, but you know it is an honor to be there. And it is also fun to hand food out through the windows during the festa. The first three years I lived in Poderi I was not invited to help in the kitchen. The next year I was invited to cut carrots. The following year, I could do carrots and lettuce, but in fact, I wasn't even invited to 'the table.'"

"The table? What does 'the table' mean?" I asked. "It sounds like a religious experience or a rite of passage."

"Oh, but it was! There is a huge worktable in one of the rooms, and on that table the dough is made for the tortelli. About five women are lined up along the table to assist with different phases of the pasta making. It begins with a great mound of flour, and I was allowed to watch as Ridova, the main pasta maker, broke one, two, three—up to twenty-six eggs into the well of the flour. She beat them up, and before our very eyes, she created a ball of pasta. That type of work is so physically hard to do, and with the amounts of pasta needed, it is even more difficult. Pinches of the dough are handed down to the next woman, who puts them through a roller-type pasta machine, a number 4, then passes them down to the next woman, who does the same on a number 2, all the time making the dough thinner and thinner. The next woman takes the ricotta mixture and places small amounts on to the pasta, and then they create the tortelli.

"As for me, I was putting the completed tortelli onto the trays and into the freezer. And they would go through this routine every day of the festa, for the pasta must be made from scratch every single day. When people came to the festa, they knew they better put in their order for tortelli quickly because they tended to run out within the first two hours. And then there were just fried potatoes and gnocchi. But everyone is aware of this, so they just get there early."

"That's some impressive job you women were doing," Win said, settling farther into his chair. I could tell he was enjoying these conversations.

"Oh, that it was. The women would get up at 5:00 a.m. in the morning to prepare the tortelli, so they would have fresh tortelli every twenty-four hours, along with the fresh pasta sauce. It took quite a bit of dedication for the women to be able to do this year after year after year. The principle cooks worked at this for ten to fifteen years, assisted by their daughters. The rest of us could work, and Margarita was allowed to work for many years despite being an 'outsider' from Germany. But they know they don't have many people to participate anymore, so they are not quite as 'ingrown' as in the past. Then, when the festa is over, the women invest the profits into a group trip and get a bus, and whoever wants to go to town with them can go. . . such as up to Frascasi, to the natural caverns with stalactites and stalagmites, or to see a famous church in another district." She sighed.

"I'm so glad we were able to attend the festa when we did," I said. "It was life transforming for me. I have been on the trail of learning about these age-old traditions ever since. I thank you personally for that opportunity, Lisa."

Win nodded in agreement. "Yes," he said, "she's never been the same. It was like a flame was lit inside, and a passion has risen up from that place."

"I'm only glad it worked out so well," Lisa said. "I look forward to seeing where this leads you."

"Me too!" I said. "Me too!" I was a bit surprised by Win's comment, but knew it was true. I just didn't realize it showed. "So, what came next after the festa?" I asked.

"Well, they always have a post-festa dinner, which is open to the community, where they eat all the leftover food—or what there is left. I believe the year you were there, you were in Firenze at the time. But we all simply eat and enjoy ourselves, while talking about how much money was made.

"One year, when we went to one of these, I remember Niccolo was about ten or eleven and running around with his friends, talking and carrying on. And Raimondo, who had been the mayor of the town six or seven years before, stood up to speak to the people in the room. He had an incredibly low, low voice but was a very authoritative person. He and his brothers were the main organizers of this festa. As he began to speak, Niccolo was yelling to his friend, and quietly Raimondo told him to take his seat. Niccolo took one look at him and sat right down, because he knew and respected Raimondo.

"It was in that moment that I became aware that this really was more than community—it was family—and it was a time and place where remonstration could be handed out because we were family, altogether. In his own way, Raimondo had said that we are members of a family, and we have responsibility to the family. Even now, when I go back, or even if I don't go back, I will hear from someone who sends their greeting because my house is still there—my place in the family is still there, and they let me know that my presence is missed."

"That's lovely, Lisa. Rarely do we experience that sense of community back here in the US," I lamented. Lisa nodded.

"I think it's, too, because everyone knows that things change —times pass, and yet there is an inherent recognition that though all of these things change, they still connect us. I remember Raimondo was saying that we need to celebrate being together *today*. The more we can see that and not be afraid of it, the better off we are. And I believe that the concept of 'spirit,' which is integrated into their beliefs about death, makes them that much stronger. It's a part of everyone; it's a celebration of life. Even though their religion includes the fear of passage into death and the acknowledgment of it, there is still a way of living well. It comes in being together and following rules because rules can give us freedom."

"That makes sense," Win said. "But it also sounds a bit tricky."

"I believe it is because cultural traditions are so endemic. For them, it is opening up your society to everyone who wants to come for the pleasure of everyone eating together—that good spirit of sharing food at the festival—which is a lovely sentiment and the way the Italians do everything!"

"You mentioned community and the acceptance of Margarita even though she was an outsider. But how accepting are the people of Poderi to people coming in from the outside for the festival?"

"I think completely; they are very accepting because they are very interested in *lo straniero,* or the stranger. They do not create separate categories for the German, the American, and the Florentine—they have a very human, amused curiosity about everyone. They are very welcoming people with an enormous well of hospitality. And that truly comes from the fact that they are only two generations away from people who knew what it was like to live without a money economy and the precious value of land and having their own place. The pride of . . . No, it's much deeper than pride.

"For example, did you happen to meet Pariso and Nina?"

Two blank looks turned toward her. Lisa shrugged and continued.

"Well, they are an older couple, perhaps seventy-five years old at the time of your visit, and are farmers who live only a hundred yards or so down the road from my house. He is a remarkable old guy, and we made a point of buying fresh produce and everything we could from them. Once when Niccolo was told by his second-grade teacher, 'You all have to go . . .' She was totally a fascist teacher, from a socialist family, but still totally fascist. Why, she would rap the kids on their heads with her big ruler and was a terribly oppressive teacher, and probably the reason why my child is not in college today. . . . . But I digress, because then she had plenty of material to work with there."

I knew there was an entirely different story here, but, at that point, I did not interrupt her.

"Anyway," Lisa said, "the teacher said to her class, 'You all must go home and interview your great-grandfather and bring your assignment back next week. And you must ask them these five questions: What was life like when you were a young child? What did you eat? Etcetera. So, Niccolo came home from second grade and asked, 'Do we have a great-grandfather?' 'No, he's dead,' I said, 'he died about fifty years ago.' So he went back the next day to report in, and the teacher said, 'It doesn't matter if you don't have one. Go find one!'

"So these poor kids were going around town trying to find a great-grandfather. So we decided to go down to interview Parisio. And Parisio was so proud to be interviewed and to have this little guy interview him. And Niccolo was so proud to be interviewing him, and their interaction was so beautiful!

"Niccolo asked him, 'Now, what did you buy with your money?' And Parisio would say, 'Well, son, we didn't have money. No, son, we had no money.' Niccolo's eyes widened at this encounter, as these two worldviews collided. My son's life was centered on a moneyed economy, and he knew absolutely what he wanted and what he needed.

"Parisio explained, 'Well, I took a piece of leather down to the general store—that was where you ate, met folks, exchanged news and merchandise, and it was also the social center of town. And I got a pound of wheat, and brought it home to make my bread. I would get some oil there for exchange for some work if they needed anything to be done; it was how we exchanged things. In those days, it was called *baratto*.'

"'How do you spell that word?' Niccolo would ask, and Parisio would carefully spell it out for him. So there was this wonderful exchange about these different eras, and to see that my child could be so fascinated—well, maybe not fascinated, but relating to this wonderful person who we loved so much and was an important part of our lives and transcribing things that were so incredible. All these were things we had never known about Parisio's life.

"The next question was, 'How did you get to work?' 'Well, we walked to work then. We didn't have a bicycle and we carried our spade on our shoulder and we walked twenty to thirty miles each day, worked all day, and then walked back home at night. We didn't have our own land, you see.'

"So that perspective of their history is still very present in their lives. And it is part of that great hospitality that we always felt and still feel there. You could never be made to feel unwelcome as a foreigner. Their doors are always open.

"'Oh, would you like to buy some oil?' Lisa continued her monologue. 'Oh, you come home with me afterwards, for we can arrange that.' They are not overly generous, but if there is interest, 'we can arrange that,' they will say. And they are very, very amenable to those who are interested in them, because they themselves are interested in other people. Many of them lived in Yugoslavia during the war, or in Germany. They traveled because their government (Mussolini) sent them out, and you will find Yugoslavian books in their homes although they only speak Italian.

"But, they have also a great innate curiosity and this is what I love about that generation of Parisio's—for they are so wise, so intelligent, and they have a great sense of irony. And throughout history, they have had a skepticism about how things work in the world. So with their ability to fit into their own land and their society, there is so much to learn by just watching and listening to them talk about how things are done and how things were done in the past. For instance, in the creation of Parisio's house, they needed to dig wells, which meant that they needed to cope with the authorities who said you can't dig wells, and then, of course, he was able to do it, anyway.

"There is an enormously creative and ingenious sense that resides here, and it extends to people when they come to visit their town. They are curious, they are interested—and they can retire back into their own space when it is appropriate to do so. It is a hospitality, a social propriety—yet not to be overly done. So, there is not a great disparity between the tourists and the actual folks living in the community. But the people who live there are carriers of a great culture, and they know that and are proud of that!"

"When it comes to getting wells dug or 'working with the government'—'greasing the wheels of government,' so to speak, do people learn to do that naturally in Italy?" Win asked.

"Common sense rules in Italy, at least in a social sense," Lisa said. "But when they are coping with a political system that is not feasible and doesn't give them enough economic space to create change, then, of course, there is a lot of dialogue going on and a lot of skepticism and a lot of perception and thinking, and eventually action. Even from that seventy-five-year-old who did not go past elementary school, who is a fine thinker and has a lot of basic logic that most of us don't really carry around with us all the time. He knows how to deal when he gets thrown a big problem. Yes, I would say he is learned.

"Many of these people have been in wars, so they learned the hard way how to negotiate and deal with life circumstances. We even had fascists down at the corner of the provincial road and Poderi's road who, during WWII, had made an encampment and were holding a central command. So in our town, of whom Raimondo and his brother Didio (who organized our festa) had parents, there was a scuffle with some of these fascists right there in our piazza in 1941 or '42. And someone was killed there, someone who was a partisan, and at the time, was under attack."

Win and my eyebrows raised. "Partisans?" I asked.

"Oh, yes, the partisans, at that time, were fighting three types of war: a civil war against the fascists, a war of liberation against the Germans, and a class war against the wealthy. A busy lot.

"But this incident in our area was considered a recent event —and that was in everybody's heart and, even now, they still know exactly who the sympathizers were. Yet all these guys, like Raimondo and Didio, are still living near here, and their aunts, uncles, and sisters are all still here. They move around, they know each other, and they co-exist. So, you do not hear these stories very often unless, of course, you ask someone specifically about these events. And then you will hear these most amazing stories.

"I am so fascinated by this period—it was a time of great uncertainty in the world and that is where the *real* humanity resides in terms of how we cope with these things—peasant, count, fascist, or Nazi. It is at that point we are all so human, and we work this out at midnight."

I took a long breath. This was quite a powerful statement to ingest, but I agreed with her, "You're so right. This is fascinating. I, too, would love to know more about the history and what life was like during World War II." My brain was whirring with ideas.

"Well, what I do know is that all of these things I mentioned before are present in Montemerano right now. And that is what is so important: to tell people the stories so younger generations will understand the great sacrifices made for them and for their families. My friend Barbara, who was raised near Salerno, told me that her family always told stories about her grandfather, just so the family would understand the great struggle and sacrifices he made in the name of his values. You see, he refused to go along with the fascist government before World War II and he lost everything—was stripped of everything. Still, he stood strong and refused to fight with them, and that, we believe, is basically what brought Italy to become a democracy because those are the very values he was fighting for."

Both Winston and I sat there, in awe of all that Lisa had laid out like a fine banquet on a time-worn table of historical understanding. We were speechless.

She interrupted our silence. "We live and believe and accept that we are in a democracy here in the US, but what it costs to keep it, and what it costs to live without it—we need to hear these very stories. Our young people need to hear these stories, so they can appreciate what they have."

Winston and I agreed. We in the US are naïve about what costs have been paid for our democracy and we, too, need to take a deeper look at our own history.

So, if you have wondered why I have chosen to write about the family stories along with the traditions and foods in France and

Italy in my *Savoring the Olde Ways* series, this interview with Lisa is one of the reasons. That small pilot light of a flame that Lisa had helped to light inside, became a bonfire of desire to understand why and how families are able to stay together and maintain their traditions. I found that these delicate secrets are discovered within their rich, and sometimes devastating, history.

FINI

RECIPES *from* *the* CHAPTERS

Lombardy

CHAPTER ONE
Vitella Picatta con Limone e Capperi Milano
(Veal Piccata with Lemon and Capers)

Serves 8

Ingredients

2 lbs. veal cutlets, pounded to 1/4-inch thickness – (also known as veal scaloppini)

1/2 cup flour (add in 1/2 teaspoon of salt and 1/4 teaspoon of pepper)

4 tablespoons of olive oil

2 tablespoons butter

1 cup veal or chicken stock – (homemade, if available)

1/2 cup white wine

2 medium lemons – (1 squeezed for juice; 1 thinly sliced)

2 tablespoons small caper berries – (if packed in salt, rinse them first)

2 tablespoons chopped fresh Italian parsley

Salt and pepper to taste

Directions

Begin by placing a large platter into your warming oven. Then, dredge the thin cutlets in the seasoned flour. Tap excess flour off. Heat the olive oil and butter together in a large skillet. Briefly sauté the scaloppini until golden brown. Remove veal to a plate and add the stock and wine to the pan. Gently simmer the liquid while stirring the bits of browned veal from the bottom. Reduce the heat and add the veal back into the pan. Cover and simmer on low for 10 minutes. Add the capers, parsley and juice from one whole lemon; simmer for 5 more minutes, then taste the sauce. Adjust seasonings, if needed. Serve veal piccata on a large warmed platter with the sauce spooned over the top and thin slices of lemon fanned out over the dish. *Deliziosa!*

Tuscany

CHAPTER TWO
Gnocchi for the Festa
(Homemade Gnocchi)

Serves 6

Ingredients

2 lbs. russet potatoes, scrubbed
1 1/2 cups of unbleached all-purpose flour, plus more
  for rolling

2 large eggs, beaten

1 teaspoon sea salt

Directions

Preheat the oven to 400°F. Pierce the potatoes with a fork. Place the potatoes into the oven and bake until tender, about 1 hour. Set aside until cool enough to handle. Take each warm potato with an oven mitt, and carefully peel the potatoes. Then place the potatoes into a potato ricer or food mill over a large bowl and let cool for about 20 minutes more.

In a small bowl, mix the flour with the salt. Drizzle the eggs into the potatoes and then add the flour mixture. Mix with your hands until the flour is moistened, and the dough starts to clump together; the dough will still be a bit crumbly at this point.

Lightly flour a work surface. Gather the dough together and place it onto the floured space. Knead until you have a smooth, cohesive dough. Takes about 2 minutes. If the dough feels sticky, sprinkle more flour onto the mass and continue to work it into the dough. Set the dough aside, covered with a kitchen towel and allow to rest for twenty minutes.

Clean the work surface, then sprinkle with more flour. Place the dough onto the surface, and with a bench scraper, cut the dough into fourths. Roll each portion into a long rope, about 3/4-inch in diameter and with the bench scraper or a sharp knife cup the rope into 3/4-inch-long pieces.

You can use a gnocchi maker to press grooves into the pasta pillows. Or use a table fork by placing the tines of the fork lightly onto each gnocchi rolling the dough toward you. (The tines form ridges on the gnocchi to better hold the pasta sauce.) Set the gnocchi onto a lightly floured parchment sheet and cover with a kitchen towel to rest. If the gnocchi is to be used right away, leave on the table until you are ready to boil them in salted water.

Bring a large pot of heavily salted water, to boil on high heat. Lifting the parchment, slide about one-third of the gnocchi into the water. Stir slightly. Add the rest the pasta, again one-third at a time. When all the gnocchi float to the top of the water, cook for another minute then, with a slotted spoon scoop them off into a bowl. Add your favorite tomato meat sauce or butter/sage sauce. But always grate plenty of Parmigiano Reggiano over the top.

CHAPTER THREE

Pappardelle al Cinghiale

(Pasta with Wild Boar Sauce)

Serves 6–8

Ingredients

2 large cloves of garlic, chopped
2 yellow onions, chopped
1 sprig fresh rosemary, chopped
1 stalk celery, chopped

1 dried chili pepper or ¼ tsp. chili flakes
6 tablespoons extra-virgin olive oil
1 1/2 lbs. coarsely ground wild boar (or pork loin)
1 cup of chianti wine
1 1/2 cups tomatoes, chopped
2 cups water
Salt and pepper to taste
2 tablespoons parsley, chopped

Directions

Lightly sauté the garlic, onions, rosemary, celery and chili pepper in the oil; add the ground wild boar and continue to sauté. Add the tomatoes and wine and simmer for 10 minutes; add the water, 1 cup at a time. Cover and cook over low heat or in a Crock Pot for up to 2 hours. Taste once again for seasonings and adjust. Cook the pasta to al dente, drain, and add to sauce. Toss until the noodles are well coated. Serve on a large warmed platter, with freshly grated Parmigiano Reggiano and a sprinkling of chopped Italian parsley

CHAPTER FOUR
Tortelli di Zucca – Pitigliano
(Butternut Squash-Filled Pasta with Butter Sage Sauce)

Serves 6–8

Ingredients for Tortelli Filling

2 lbs. of butternut squash
1/2 cup of amaretti cookies, finely crushed (make

certain to measure out a full 1/2 cup of cookies *before* crushing)
1/2 cup grated parmesan cheese
1/2 cup *mostarda* (spicy pears and apples compote from Lombardy)
Nutmeg, salt and pepper, to taste
Breadcrumbs (if needed)

Note: *Mostarda* is a piquant condiment made from candied fruits, vinegar, mustard, and spices. If you cannot source (Amazon approx. $15–$20), you can substitute using wholegrain mustard, red chili flake, and a small amount of applesauce. It will not be a perfect trade and you will need to experiment to get your favorite blend; however, from research, I have found there are many variations of *Mostarda*, and as we know, every Italian grandma has the best recipe! [Steve Higgs, chef and recipe tester]

Peach-Apricot Mostarda Recipe

1 cup of apricot jam
1/2 teaspoon ginger powder
1 teaspoon dried mustard
1/2 teaspoon salt
1/8 teaspoon pepper
1 teaspoon mustard
2 teaspoon vinegar (apple cider, or white wine)

Simmer in a small pan to cook the Mostarda down, for about 10 minutes. (Martha Engber)

Directions for Filling

Cut open your butternut squash, cut it into large chunks, remove seeds and fibers with a spoon. Roast the squash in a 350°F oven for about 45 minutes, or until the flesh is quite tender when pricked with a fork. Let the squash cool, turning it over to allow any excess liquid to drain out. (If the pumpkin pieces seem watery, wrap them in cheesecloth and squeeze dry.) Scrape away the cooked flesh from the skin into a food processor. Add the amaretti, parmesan and *mostarda*, and process until you have a perfectly smooth, stiff paste.

Season the mixture generously with freshly grated nutmeg, fresh ground pepper and salt. If the mixture is too soft or wet, mix in some breadcrumbs, a little at a time, until the stuffing is stiff and holds together well. Cool.

Ingredients for Fresh Tortelli

2 cups unbleached all-purpose flour
3 large eggs, room temperature, and lightly beaten

Directions for Making Tortelli

Sift flour onto a clean work surface and form a mountain. Make a well in the center of the mountain and pour the beaten eggs into the center. Using a fork, stir the eggs into the flour from the center of the well, by incorporating more and more flour until the dough is soft and begins to stick together. Approximately 3 minutes. If the dough is too dry, add a drop or two of water. Transfer the dough onto a lightly floured surface and knead the dough until it becomes satiny, about 10 to 15 minutes. Cover with a clean kitchen towel and allow to rest for 1 hour.

Having allowed the dough to rest for 1 hour, divide the dough into four parts. Keep three of those sections covered with the kitchen towel, while you work on the first section. Follow the directions on your pasta machine to process the dough to form the thinnest sheets possible. This recipe rolls to a #2 and produces 50 pieces.

Lightly flour a workspace and while using a 3-inch round biscuit cutter, cut as many circles into the dough as possible. Taking the bowl of pumpkin filling and a clean teaspoon, place a spoonful of filling into the middle of the pasta circle. Do not overfill. Fold the circle into halves. Dip your fingers into a cup of water and moisten the edges to stick it together. Take the corners of the *mezza luna* (half moon shape) and pull the corners together to touch and pinch them together lightly. Once they've been formed, lightly dust the tortelli with flour and place them on a parchment sheet on top of a baking sheet. Don't let the tortelli touch once formed.

When you've made the filled pasta, bring a large pot of water to a boil and add a tablespoon or two of sea salt. Bring back to a second boil and, with a slotted spoon lower the Tortelli into the water a few at a time. Stir the pot occasionally to prevent the pasta from sticking on the bottom of the pot or to each other. Cook until all the Tortelli has risen to the surface of the pot, about 5 minutes. Taste one for doneness. Serve in a warmed serving bowl with your favorite butter sage sauce.

Ingredients for Sage Butter Sauce

8 tablespoons of unsalted butter
12 medium fresh sage leaves
1/4–1/2 cup of pecorino or parmigiana cheese
1 lemon

Directions for Sage Butter Sauce

Prepare the sage butter sauce by melting the butter on very low heat in a small saucepan. Stack the sage leaves on top of each other and with a sharp knife, cut the stack into thin strips. Swirl them into the butter and keep them warm, but do not continue to heat. (The sage will taste bitter.)

Pour over the tortelli, and grate pecorino or parmigiana cheese over the top. Micro plane and zest the lemon over the dish before tossing. It will add a light, bright flavor and help to cut any extra sweetness from the filling.

CHAPTER FIVE

Cinghiale – Manciano

(Wild Boar Roast)

Serves 6–8

Ingredients

1 medium onion, chopped into 1-inch chunks
4 cloves garlic – (mince 2 of the cloves)
2 medium carrots, chopped into 1-inch chunks

2 medium celery stalks, chopped into 1-inch chunks
1 cup fennel, chopped into 1-inch chunks
1/2 cup olive oil, divided
Salt and pepper to taste
2–3 lbs. wild boar roast (or pork roast)
5 sprigs, fresh thyme, finely chopped
3 sprigs, fresh rosemary, finely chopped
1 tablespoon, fresh oregano leaves
3 sprigs of sage, finely chopped
1/2–3/4 cups of water

Directions

Set oven to 375° degrees. Toss the chopped vegetables (including onion, two garlic cloves, celery, fennel) in 1/4 cup of olive oil. Layer the vegetables in the bottom of a roasting pan.

Season the roast with salt and pepper. Heat a skillet with a tablespoon of olive oil and add the roast to sear on all sides. Place the roast onto the vegetables in the roasting pan.

In a small bowl, add the finely chopped herbs, the chopped garlic and the rest of the olive oil. With a spoon, stir the mixture into a paste. Then rub the herbal paste over the roast. Add the water to the bottom of the pan and roast in the oven until a meat thermometer reached 155–160°F or about 1 hour. Allow to rest about 5 minutes before slicing. Arrange the cinghiale (roast boar) on a warmed platter surrounded with the roasted vegetables.

CHAPTER SIX
Aquacotta – Sovana
(Peasant-Style Vegetable Soup)

Serves 4

Ingredients

6 tablespoons extra virgin olive oil, divided
2 cloves of garlic, green germ removed, peeled
3 stalks of celery, medium diced (1/2")
2 onions, medium diced (1/2")
19 oz. can of Cento San Marzano crushed tomatoes
1/8 teaspoon red chili pepper flakes
1 tablespoon of Italian seasoning
Salt and pepper to taste
8 slices of day-old bread
4 eggs
1/2 cup of Parmigiano Reggiano cheese, freshly grated

Directions

In a saucepan or large cast iron pot, sauté one clove of garlic, lightly crushed, with 4 tablespoons of extra virgin olive oil, then add the diced vegetables, crushed tomatoes, chili pepper flakes, Italian seasoning, and a good pinch of salt. Let cook for a few minutes, stirring with a wooden spoon, then add 2 quarts of hot water. Simmer the covered pot on the lowest heat for about 2 hours and a half. Check the simmer.

When the soup is almost ready, broil the bread slices, then rub them with a clove of garlic and tear them into pieces with your hands, distributing the bread at the bottom of 4 soup bowls.

Carefully, break each egg into a cup, one at a time, and gently ease it into the pot where the soup is still simmering, taking care not to break the yolk. As soon as the egg whites are firm, remove the eggs with a slotted spoon and keep them warm in a dish.

Distribute the soup into soup bowls over the bread slices. Very carefully place one egg in the center of each bowl and season with a drizzle of extra virgin olive oil and top with a generous sprinkling of grated Parmigiano Reggiano cheese. Serve hot.

CHAPTER SEVEN
Bistecca alla Fiorentina
(Porterhouse Steak, Florence Style)

Serves 4 (Two Steaks)

Ingredients

2 2 lb. Porterhouse Steaks, specially cut to 2 inches thick
1/2 teaspoon black pepper, coarsely ground
1/2 teaspoon sea salt, coarsely ground
3-4 tablespoons of good extra-virgin olive oil – Tuscan, if available
3 tablespoons of aged-balsamic Vinegar
1/8 cup fresh rosemary sprigs, chopped
3–4 fresh sprigs of rosemary, whole
1 Meyer Lemon, cut in half

Directions

Remove the steaks from the refrigerator and place them on a plate or a sheet of parchment paper. Sprinkle the coarsely ground pepper and sea salt over both sides of both steaks and press into the meat. Drizzle olive oil and a little balsamic vinegar over the meat, then press chopped rosemary into the surface with the seasonings and allow to rest for at least 30–60 minutes before grilling.

Prepare the grill. Place the steaks onto the hot grill with several sprigs of rosemary and grill for about five to six minutes per side for medium rare. Place lemon halves on upper rack to warm. Turn steak every couple of minutes. Remove the rosemary to an upper rack after about five minutes and place lemon directly onto the grill. Place steaks onto a carving board to rest for a few minutes before slicing into 1/4" slices. Squeeze the lemon halves over the meat and serve with a sprig of fresh rosemary on the steak.

CHAPTER EIGHT

Tiramisu

(Brandy & Espresso-Flavored Spongecake)

Ingredients

6 large egg yolks
3/4 cup white sugar
3/4 cup whole milk
4 8-ounce containers of mascarpone cheese, room temp

1 1/2 cups espresso or strong black coffee, at room
  temperature
1/2 cup brand or cognac
30–32 crisp Italian ladyfingers
1/4 cup Dutch-process cocoa powder
Bittersweet chocolate for shaving over top

Directions

Set out an 8-inch-square baking dish. Fill a large bowl
with ice water.

Make the custard: Whisk the egg yolks and sugar in the
top of a double-boiler over barely simmering water
until the sugar dissolves. Slowly whisk in the milk and
cook, whisking constantly, until the custard is light and
foamy, about 15–20 minutes (it takes time).

Remove the double-boiler top from the bottom of the
double-boiler and set in the bowl of ice water; whisk
until the custard is cool, about 1 minute. Put the
mascarpone in a large bowl. Fold the custard into the
mascarpone with a rubber spatula until almost
combined, then whisk until just smooth (do not
overmix or the custard will be grainy).

Combine the espresso and brandy in a shallow bowl.
One at a time, dip the ladyfingers in the espresso
mixture until soaked but not soggy; arrange 2 rows of
about 5 biscuits each in the baking dish. Spread one-
third of the mascarpone custard over the ladyfingers.
Repeat with a second layer of espresso-dipped
ladyfingers, arranging them in the opposite direction.
Top with another one-third of the custard. Repeat with

the remaining ladyfingers, alternating directions. Spread the remaining custard on top and dust with the cocoa powder. Cover with plastic wrap; refrigerate at least 4 hours, or overnight. Remove the plastic wrap. Shave curls of chocolate on top with a vegetable peeler. Cut into serving size portions and serve.

CHAPTER NINE
Minestra di Verdura Passata
(Puréed Vegetable Soup)

Serves 8

Ingredients

12 ounces canned cannellini beans
1/2 cup olive oil, divided
1/2 medium yellow onion, chopped
1 clove garlic, minced
1/2 cup tomato sauce
1 fresh sprig parsley
2 carrots, chopped
1 celery stalk, chopped
4 medium potatoes, cut into 1-inch chunks
2 medium zucchinis, cut into 1-inch chunks
1 cup fresh or frozen peas
6–9 cups good chicken or vegetable broth (homemade, if available)
Salt and pepper to taste
Toasted sliced Italian bread, rubbed with garlic

Directions

In a stock pot, heat 1/4 cup of olive oil and sauté the chopped onion for about 5 minutes over medium heat. Add the clove of garlic and continue to sauté for another 2 minutes. Then, add the tomato sauce and sprig of parsley and cook 10 minutes more. Then, add the rest of the olive oil and all the vegetables except the peas to the pot. Cook for another 10 minutes. Add the peas and the broth, cover and simmer on low heat for 45 minutes.

In the food processor or blender, add the vegetable soup and purée until smooth. Return the soup to the pot, bring to a boil then serve in soup bowls with bread slices floated on the top.

CHAPTER TEN

Limoncello Digestivo, Poderi di Montemerano
(Lemon Digestive)

Makes Ten Cups

Ingredients

12 large fresh lemons
4 cups + 2 ounces of plain vodka or grain alcohol
4 cups + 2 ounces of water
3 2/3 cups sugar

Directions

After thoroughly scrubbing all the lemons, dry and with a vegetable peeler, remove only the yellow outsides of the lemon. No pith! Place the peelings in a large glass jar (about 1-1/2 quarts) and add the alcohol. Store in a cool dark place for seven to ten days. As for the lemon juice, squeeze all of it into a measuring cup and pour into ice cube trays to freeze for use in other recipes.

Remove from the dark place and discard the peelings. Filter them from the liquid using a coffee filter. (Use several filters to keep the process flowing—a slow process, at best.) Bring water to a boil. Add sugar, dissolve. Stir, then set aside to cool completely. Add the lemon alcohol to sugar water. Pour liquid into individual bottles and store in freezer. Serve directly from the freezer into small glasses. Enjoy! [Kathy Grossenbacher]

Campania

CHAPTER ELEVEN

Pizza Margherita – Naples
(Original Neapolitan Pizza)

Makes One 8-Inch Pizza

Ingredients for Pizza Dough

1 teaspoon active dry yeast
1 teaspoon sugar
1 1/4 cups lukewarm water
2 tablespoons extra-virgin olive oil
1 teaspoon fine sea salt
3 3/4 cups of bread flour
Course cornmeal

Ingredients for Margherita Pizza

1 large fresh tomato, thinly sliced
1 ball of buffalo mozzarella, sliced
1/8 cup of olive oil
1 tablespoon of crumbled leaf oregano
Five or six fresh basil leaves

Directions

In a large bowl, combine the yeast, sugar, and water, and stir to blend. Let stand until foamy, about 5 minutes. Sir in the oil and salt.

Add the flour, a little at a time, stirring until most of the flour has been absorbed and the dough forms a ball. Transfer the dough to a floured work surface and knead until soft and smooth yet still firm, about 4-5 minutes. Add additional flour as needed to keep the dough from sticking.

Transfer the dough to a bowl, cover tightly with Saran wrap, and place in the refrigerator. Let the dough rise in the refrigerator until double or tripled in bulk, about 8 to 12 hours. Simply punch down the dough as it doubles and triples. Proceed with the individual pizza recipes.

About 40 minutes before placing assembled pizzas into an oven, preheat the oven to 500°F. If using a pizza stone preheat the stone. Punch down the dough and divide into fourths. Shape each fourth into a ball. On a lightly floured surface, roll each ball of dough into an 8-inch round less than 1-inch thick.

Sprinkle a pizza peel or baking sheet with coarse

cornmeal and place the rounds on the peel or the sheet. Working quickly to keep the dough from sticking, assemble the pizzas. For Pizza Margherita, brush the dough with olive oil, then top with concentric circles of thinly sliced fresh tomatoes and mozzarella cheese. Drizzle a bit more olive oil over the top and sprinkle with crumbled leaf oregano.

Slide the pizzas off the peel and onto the baking stone or pizza pan. Bake until the dough is crisp and golden, or about 10 to 15 minutes. After cutting into slices, add a few fresh basil leaves before serving. *Buon appetito!* [Patricia Wells' *Trattoria*]

CHAPTER TWELVE
Risotto al Pescatore – Amalfi
(Seafood Risotto)

To prepare a fine risotto with sea food, you must begin by making a good fish stock. You can make this ahead of time and use fish, shrimp, clam or mussel shells in combination to make a good flavorful stock.

Serves 6–8

Ingredients for Fish Stock

2 lbs. fish trimmings, preferably cod, bass, halibut, or
   even shrimp, crab, or clam shells
10 cups cold water
1 large onion, chopped
3 carrots, chopped

10 fennel seeds
1 bay leaf
5 peppercorns
3 tablespoons parsley, chopped
2 cups white wine

Directions for Fish Stock

Cover the fish trimmings in a large pot with the cold water. Bring to a boil and skim off any foam. Turn off the heat, let rest, and skim again. Measure 5 1/2 cups of stock into a second pan and add the rest of the ingredients. Cook at a low simmer for 30 minutes. Taste stock for flavor.

Ingredients for Seafood Risotto

2 lbs. prawns
2 lbs. calamari
3 lbs. clams, well-scrubbed
1/4 cup olive oil
1/4 cup butter
1 onion, finely minced
2 cups Arborio rice
3/4 cup of white wine
1/2 peperoncino (dried red chile), seeded and finely
  chopped
2 cloves garlic, minced
4 tablespoons parsley, minced
1/4 cup water (from cooked clams)
2/3 lb. of fresh tomatoes, finely chopped
2 fresh lemons, cut into wedges
Plenty of salt and pepper to taste

Directions for Risotto

While the fish stock is cooking, peel and devein the prawns. Clean the calamari. Cut both prawns and calamari into thin strips. Cover and set aside. Cook the cleaned clams in 2 inches of water until they open. Do not overcook. Remove the clams, cool, and shuck them. Strain the clam water through a cheesecloth until it is clear. Set aside.

For the risotto, heat the oil and butter in a large saucepan. Add the minced onion and sauté over medium heat until translucent, about 4 to 5 minutes. Add the rice and cook long enough to coat the grains of rice, 1 to 2 minutes. Stir in 1/2 cup of white wine and cook until it evaporates. Begin adding the boiling stock 1/3 cup at a time and cook, stirring constantly, over medium heat. Risotto will take at least 20 minutes to cook. Test for al dente.

After twelve minutes of the risotto cooking, and in a separate pan, sauté the peperoncino, garlic, and half the parsley very briefly over medium-low heat. Add the remaining 1/4 cup wine and cook briefly. Stir in the calamari, prawns, and 1/4 cup reserved clam water; cook until prawns are pink, and calamari is tender. Do not overcook the seafood. About 5 to 8 minutes before the risotto is done, stir in the tomatoes, remaining parsley, the clams, and the seafood. Finish the last addition of stock. Season to taste with salt and pepper. Serve immediately before a fawning audience. [Carol Field, Celebrating Italy]

....

CHAPTER THIRTEEN
Pasta alla Vongole – Amalfi
(Pasta with Clams)

Serves 4

Ingredients

36 Littleneck or Cherrystone clams, well-scrubbed and
   cleaned of sand
1/2 cup extra-virgin olive oil, divided
2–3 large cloves of garlic, minced
4 tablespoons parsley, chopped
Freshly ground black pepper
1 lb. linguine, cooked al dente
Big pinch of crushed red pepper flakes
1/4 cup of chopped fresh Italian parsley

Directions

Place the clams in an extra-large frying pan (large
enough to accommodate the clams and all the cooked
linguine), add one half of the olive oil, put on a cover
and cook over high heat for about 6 minutes. Remove
the pan from the heat, and set aside, uncovered.

When the clams are cool enough to handle, remove
them from their shells saving the clam liquid into a
small bowl. If the clams are large, chop them into
smaller pieces. If they are small, leave them in the shell.

Put the remaining olive oil into the pan, and heat on
medium. Add the cloves of garlic, quickly stirring until
they are golden brown. Do not burn. Remove the pan

from the heat, add the clams, the reserved juices, if any, the parsley, and seasonings. Prepare the linguine, and when al dente, using a pasta spoon, scoop the hot pasta directly into the clam sauce and swirl around so all of the pasta is coated. Sprinkle the red pepper flakes on the top to taste. Serve in a heated pasta bowl/platter and sprinkle with chopped parsley. Have crusty Italian garlic bread on hand to sop up juices.

CHAPTER FOURTEEN

Caprese Salad

(Fresh Tomato, Mozzarella, and Basil Salad)

Serves 4

Ingredients

1–2 large fresh tomatoes, sliced in 1/2-inch slices
1 handful fresh basil leaves, torn
1 ball of buffalo mozzarella cheese, sliced in 1/2-inch slices
1/4 cup of good extra-virgin olive oil, from Sicily or Compania, if possible
1/8 cup of aged balsamic vinegar
Freshly ground black pepper and sea salt

Directions

On a nice narrow platter, arrange the ingredients down the plate by alternating them, tomato slice, cheese slice, then basil leaf. Drizzle the olive oil over the top, then the balsamic vinegar. Sprinkle liberally with freshly ground black pepper and sea salt. Serve immediately.

Apulia

··

CHAPTER FIFTEEN

Involtini di Melanzane – Apulia
(Baked Cheese-Stuffed Eggplant)

These *involtini* are versatile and can be served as an appetizer, a side dish, or a vegetarian main course. Serve them hot out of the oven or let stand until they are just warm.

Serves 4 Main Course or 8 Appetizer Servings

Ingredients

2 large eggplants (2 lbs. total)
Sea salt
1/2 cup extra virgin olive oil, divided in two
6–8 ounces of mozzarella or scamorza cheese
6–8 ounces of pecorino fresco, or Asiago fresco, or a
  combination
3–4 ounces freshly grated Parmigiano-Reggiano
2 cups chopped mushrooms
1 1/2 to 2 cups of homemade tomato sauce, heated
  through

Directions

Remove the tops and bottoms from the eggplants and discard them. With either a mandoline or a sharp knife, carefully cut the eggplant lengthwise into 1/4-inch thick slices. (You should have 8 slices from each eggplant for a total of 16 slices). Salt the eggplant slices on both sides and layer them on a paper towel-lined rimmed baking sheet, or layered in a large colander. Let them sit for 1 hour, then pat them dry.

Heat the oven to 400°F. Line two rimmed baking sheets with parchment. Brush the eggplant slices on both sides with half the olive oil and arrange them in a single layer on the baking sheets, 8 per sheet. Bake for 10 minutes; turn the slices over and bake for 10 minutes more, until they are tender and lightly browned. (You can bake them one sheet at a time, or both sheets at once, on racks placed in the top and center of the oven.) Let the slices cool while you prepare the filling. Reduce the oven heat to 375°F.

Cut the scamorza or mozzarella (if using) into small cubes. Shred the pecorino or Asiago on the large holes of a box grater. Combine the cheeses in a bowl and stir in the Parmigiano. In a small saucepan, lightly sauté the mushrooms in the rest of the oil. Set aside to cool.

Mix the mushrooms into the cheese. Then, lightly coat an 8-inch by 11-inch rectangular baking dish with olive oil. Spoon about 1/3 cup of tomato sauce into the bottom of the dish. Place a spoonful of the cheese filling on the wide end of one of the eggplant slices. Roll it up and set it in the baking dish, seam side down. Stuff and roll up the remaining eggplant slices and place them in the dish, taking care to reserve about 1/2 cup of the filling. The involtini should fit snugly in the dish. Spoon the remaining tomato sauce on top of the involtini, and top with the remaining cheese.

Bake the involtini, uncovered, for 30 to 40 minutes, until the filling oozes and the top is browned in spots.

Let sit for 5 minutes before serving and serve hot or warm.

CHAPTER SIXTEEN

Orecchiette con Cime di Rapa – Porto Caesareo
(Ear-Shaped Pasta with Broccoli Rabe)

Broccoli rabe is from the broccoli family but its flavor is more bitter yet marries well with the other ingredients in this recipe. Great Fall favorite.

Serves 4

Ingredients

15-ounce package of dried orecchiette
1 bunch of broccoli rabe, roughly chopped
3 tablespoons of olive oil
1 garlic clove, finely sliced
1 small red chili, chopped
1/4 cup of pancetta, cut into thin sticks
Basil leaves, crushed into a paste with 1 teaspoon olive oil
Sea salt and freshly ground black pepper, to taste
1 heaping tablespoon Italian parsley, finely chopped
1/4 cup pecorino cheese, grated

Directions

Bring a large pot of salted water to boil, add the orecchiette, and boil for five minutes before adding the broccoli rabe. Cook for five minutes and test pasta for doneness. The broccoli rabe should still be slightly crisp.

Meanwhile, heat the olive oil in a large frying pan and add the garlic, chili and pancetta. Fry over medium heat for 1 minute, then add the homemade basil oil and season with salt and pepper.

Add the orecchiette and broccoli rabe directly to the pan from the pot and toss to coat in the oil. Add the parsley and grated pecorino to taste. Toss briefly, then remove from the stove and serve on a heated platter.

Apulia

CHAPTER SEVENTEEN
Fettuccine alla Papalina – Roma
(The Pope's Pasta)

Serves 4

Ingredients

14 ounces of fettuccine or tagliatelle, fresh or dried
1 small onion, peeled and finely chopped
1 cup of fresh shelled peas, or frozen if not in season
1 1/3 cups of cooked ham, cut into 3/4-inch cubes
1 cup heavy cream
3 large eggs
1 cup Parmigiano cheese, grated
1 tablespoon of butter/or olive oil
Salt for pasta water
Black pepper, freshly ground, to taste

Directions

Shell the fresh peas, if using, and cook them in a little boiling salted water for 10 minutes. (Fresh peas take longer to cook than frozen.) In the meantime, beat the eggs in a bowl with the grated Parmigiano.

Put a pot of water on to boil for the pasta. Add salt once it begins to boil and bring it to a boil once again before adding the pasta. In a sauté pan, cook the finely chopped onion in the butter or olive oil until translucent. Add the cooked ham to the onion and cook for a few minutes. Then, add the peas and allow the flavors to marry. If the peas are still too hard, add a little water to the sauce and cook a bit longer. Then, add the heavy cream and continue to reduce a bit. Add both ground black pepper and salt to taste.

Cook the pasta al dente according to the package directions. If fresh pasta, cook for 1 to 2 minutes. When cooked, lift the pasta directly from the pasta water into the sauté pan with a pasta spoon. Pour the beaten eggs and cheese over the hot pasta and sauce. Mix all together well until the pasta is coated in the creamy sauce. Serve immediately, with liberal sprinklings of grated cheese and freshly ground black pepper. Fit for a Pope!

CHAPTER EIGHTEEN
Pollo alla Romana – Roma
(Chicken Cacciatore, Hunter Style)

Serves 4

Ingredients

1 frying chicken, about 2 ½ pounds, cut into 8
1 1/2 tablespoons lard for frying
1 large red bell pepper, cored, seeded, and julienned
3 ounces *prosciutto*, thinly sliced and julienned
2 large garlic cloves, peeled and crushed
1 28-ounce can of crushed tomatoes (drain off some juice)
2/3 cup dry white wine
1 1/2 tablespoons fresh marjoram (or 1 teaspoon dried marjoram)
Salt and freshly ground black pepper to taste

Directions

Heat the frying pan and add the lard. When the lard begins to sizzle, add the chicken pieces and fry them until they are a golden brown. Turn them once during cooking. Add bell peppers and sauté to let them soften. Add the *prosciutto* and the garlic. When the garlic is nicely browned and smells pungent, add the tomatoes, and carefully stir everything together. Add the wine slowly so it doesn't splatter. Cook the chicken at simmer for about 5 minutes and then add the marjoram, salt and pepper. Stir again. Gently simmer for about 20 minutes more or until the chicken is done. Serve the chicken very hot and have plenty of crusty homemade bread to go with it. [Carlo Middione – The Food of Southern Italy]

CHAPTER NINETEEN
Saltimbocca alla Romana – Roma
(Veal Scallopini with Prosciutto and Sage)

Serves 4

Ingredients

4 (5-ounce) thinly sliced veal cutlets (scallopini) or pork
  or chicken tenderloin slices, if veal is not available
4 slices *prosciutto*, thinly sliced
12 fresh sage leaves
1/2 cup all-purpose flour, for dredging
Sea salt and freshly ground black pepper
2 tablespoons extra-virgin olive oil
2 tablespoons unsalted butter
2 tablespoons dry white wine
1/4 cup chicken broth
1 large lemon, cut into 8 wedges

Directions

Place the veal cutlets side-by-side on a sheet of plastic wrap. Lay a slice of prosciutto on top of each cutlet and cover with another piece of plastic. Gently flatten the cutlets with a rolling pin or meat mallet, until the pieces are 1/4-inch thick and the prosciutto and veal have adhered together. Remove the plastic wrap and lay a couple of sage leaves in the center of each cutlet. Weave a toothpick in and out of the veal to secure the prosciutto and sage. Put some flour in a shallow plate and season with a fair amount of salt and pepper; mix with a fork to combine. Dredge the veal in the seasoned flour, shaking off the excess.

Heat the olive oil and 1 tablespoon of the butter in a large skillet over medium flame. Put the veal in the pan, prosciutto-side down. Cook for 3 minutes to crisp it up and the flip the veal over and sauté the other side for two minutes, until golden. Transfer the saltimbocca to a warmed serving platter. Remove the toothpicks and keep warm.

Add the wine to the pan, stirring to bring up all the delicious flavor in the bottom. Let the wine cook down for a minute to burn off some of the alcohol. Add the chicken broth and remaining tablespoon of butter, swirl the pan around. Season with salt and pepper. Pour the sauce over the saltimbocca, garnish with sage leaves and lemon wedges; serve immediately. [Food Network, Tyler Florence]

REFERENCES

The Hilltop Towns of the Fiora Valley, Sovana: R. Bianchi Bandinelli, Rinascimento del libro, Firenze 1929.

A Traveller's History of Italy, 3rd Edition, Early Italy: From Cave-Dwellers to Etruscan Civilization by Valerio Lintner. 1995.

Pompeii and the Villa of the Mysteries, Loretta Santini, Casa Editrice Plurigraf, 1998.

Dictionary of Italian Cuisine, Maureen B. Fant & Howard M. Isaacs, Ecco Press, 1998.

Tutto Sorano, Guida Turistica, a Cura di Alberto Pellegrini, Publi Ed., s.a.s, (English Edition), 1998.

Capri, Island of Love – The Italian Islands – Casa Editrice Plurigraf, (English Edition), 1997.

*Guide to the Roman Forum * Palatine * Imperial Forums * Coliseum* – Francesco Papafava, Editoriale Museum, 1995.

Past and Present – The Colosseum – Rome – Lozzi Roma, 1998.

ACKNOWLEDGMENTS

It is with deep gratitude that I thank all those who helped to make this book, Book Three of the Savoring the Olde Ways Series, come to fruition. First of all, I want to thank my husband, Winston Bumpus, who took me "away from it all" for a month in Italy when I first retired from my career as a family therapist. This book chronicles our shared adventure to a new place and a newfound understanding of the wonderful people of Italy.

With that thought in mind, I want to especially thank Lisa Young from San Francisco, who embraced the two of us and took us by the hand to introduce us to the world of Italian cuisine and culture in a small Tuscan village called Poderi di Montemerano. (We have never been the same. Thank you, Lisa.) I want to also thank Margarita Vogel, Lisa's dear neighbor in Poderi, who welcomed us as friends and immediately immersed us in a better understanding of the world of traditional and regional Italian ways.

I want to thank my critique group, my first team of editors, who read through this book time and time again: Lucy Murray, Cheryl Ray, and Mary Ellen Hills. They have, in fact, tirelessly given me feedback for the past thirteen years, and to continue to support me through each of the five books I have brought to life. Thank you, too, to my editor, Darlene Frank, who has worked, unstintingly, on this series of three books. She has taught me to have a full appreciation of the difficult work of an editor and pushed me to lift my writing to a higher plane. Thanks also go to Sandra Whatmore and Grace Lowe, and John Pinto, who, due to their proud Italian heritage, were able to painstakingly check my Italian vernacular for accuracy, and to Steve Higgs, a good friend and corporate chef, who patiently tested the recipes and helped with substitutions for some "unknown Italian ingredients" involved. To Barb Stark-Nemon, Nancy Zmijewski, Linda Ryan, Cheryl Ray, Geri Rypkema, Margaret (Peggye) Cohen, Carolynn Ziance, Paula Cuneo, Barbara Artson, Pauline Jones, Liz Allison, Sandy Hardaker, Megan McDonald, and Martha Engber, my deep gratitude and thanks for your painstaking testing of the many Italian dishes. You gave me great insight and help when editing these recipes. To Mike Morgenfeld, my go-to cartographer and map maker for the past five books—my deepest thanks. You lend professionalism to my journeys.

To the entire She Writes Press team of publishing professionals who have worked with me, encouraged me, laughed with me, and helped me to produce all five of my books, I give you my deepest appreciation and thanks for pushing me to reach for the highest quality and integrity in this process. They include Brooke Warner, Crystal Patriarche, Lauren Wise, Shannon Green, Stacey Aaronson, and Samantha Strom. And to Caitlin Hamilton Summie Marketing and Publicity (Caitlin and Rick both), my thanks go to you for holding my hand and leading me once again through all forms of pushing my books into the world—here and abroad.

Thank you, one and all.

ABOUT THE AUTHOR

photo credit: Chris Loomis

CAROLE BUMPUS began writing about food and travel when she stumbled upon the amazing stories of women and war in France. Her historical novel, *A Cup of Redemption*, was published in October 2014, and her unique companion cookbook, *Recipes for Redemption: A Companion Cookbook to A Cup of Redemption*, was released in August 2015. Book one of her *Savoring the Olde Ways Series, Searching for Family and Traditions at the French Table*, was published in August 2019 and Book Two was published in August 2020. She has appeared on various national and international podcasts and radio shows, and she has had numerous articles and blog posts published, as well as three short stories in the Fault Zone anthologies: *Words from the Edge, Stepping up to the Edge,* and *Over the Edge*. A retired family therapist, Bumpus lives in the San Francisco Bay Area.

Visit her website at www.carolebumpus.com.

SELECTED TITLES FROM SHE WRITES PRESS

She Writes Press is an independent publishing company
founded to serve women writers everywhere.
Visit us at www.shewritespress.com.

A Cup of Redemption by Carole Bumpus. $16.95, 978-1-938314-90-2.
Three women, each with their own secrets and shames, seek to make
peace with their pasts and carve out new identities for themselves
while in France.

Searching for Family and Traditions at the French Table, Book One by
Carole Bumpus. $16.95, 978-1-63152-896-5. Part culinary memoir
and part travelogue, this compilation of intimate interviews,
conversations, stories, and traditional family recipes (*cuisine pauvre*)
in the kitchens of French families, gathered by Carole Bumpus as
she traveled throughout France's countryside, is about people
savoring the life they have been given.

Searching for Family and Traditions at the French Table, Book Two by
Carole Bumpus. $16.95, 978-1-63152-896-5. An intimate peek
inside the homes and lives of the French, a collection of traditional
French recipes, and a compendium of culinary cultural traditions,
sprinkled with historical anecdotes and spiced with humor and
deliciously candid memories, this culinary travel memoir—the
second of the Savoring the Olde Ways series—reveals French
families at their best and at their own dinner tables.

Recipes for Redemption: A Companion Cookbook to A Cup of Redemption
by Carole Bumpus. $19.95, 978-1-63152-824-8. A uniquely
character-centered cookbook that offers delicious recipes—and
savory stories—straight from the pages of *A Cup of Redemption.*

*Away from the Kitchen: Untold Stories, Private Menus, Guarded Recipes,
and Insider Tips* by Dawn Blume Hawkes. $24.95,
978-1-938314-36-0. A food book for those who want it all: the
menus, the recipes, *and* the behind-the-scenes scoop on some of
America's favorite chefs.

*Seasons Among the Vines: Life Lessons from the California Wine Country
and Paris* by Paula Moulton. $16.95, 978-1-938314-16-2. New advice
on wine making, tasting, and food pairing—along with a spirited
account of the author's experiences in Le Cordon Bleu's pilot wine
program—make this second edition even better than the first.